SCREEN ADDICTS

STRATEGIES TO COMBAT SMARTPHONE ABUSE IN CHILDREN AND ADOLESCENTS

DAVID SANDUA

"Neuroscience tells us that excessive use of screens can affect brain development in children and adolescents. It is essential to implement strategies that promote play, reading and face-to-face interaction."

Dr. Martin Velasco, pediatric neurologist.

INDEX

I. INTRODUCTION

In today's technologically advanced society, smartphones have become an integral part of our daily lives, serving as a means of communication, entertainment, and access to information. While these devices have undoubtedly brought numerous benefits, their excessive use among children and adolescents has raised concerns about potential negative effects on their development and well-being. The increasing prevalence of smartphone abuse has emerged as a pressing issue, not only among parents but also among educators, mental health professionals, and policymakers. This essay aims to explore the strategies that can be employed to combat smartphone abuse in children and adolescents. By examining the detrimental consequences of excessive smartphone use, analyzing the underlying factors contributing to this behavior, and highlighting effective interventions, this study seeks to provide insight into this pervasive problem and offer potential solutions. The goal is to equip parents, educators, and relevant stakeholders with knowledge and tools necessary to address smartphone abuse and promote healthy technology use among the younger generation.

SMARTPHONE ABUSE IN CHILDREN AND ADOLESCENTS

Smartphone abuse in children and adolescents can be defined as the excessive and compulsive use of smartphones that negatively impacts their physical, mental, and social well-being. It encompasses behaviors such as spending substantial amounts of time on smartphones, neglecting important tasks and responsibilities, experiencing difficulties in controlling smartphone usage, and deriving pleasure and satisfaction from using smartphones. The widespread availability and accessibility of smartphones, coupled with the proliferation of apps, games, and social media platforms, have created an environment that fosters dependency and addiction among young individuals. Smartphone abuse is characterized by a loss of self-regulation and an inability to moderate usage, leading to a range of adverse consequences. These consequences may include impaired academic performance, disrupted sleep patterns, decreased physical activity, strained interpersonal relationships, heightened anxiety and depression, and a diminished ability to concentrate and focus on tasks. Smartphone abuse can also contribute to the development of addictive behaviors and disorders, such as Internet addiction and gaming addiction. Given the alarming prevalence of smartphone abuse among children and adolescents, it is crucial to address this issue proactively and implement strategies to combat and mitigate its detrimental effects.

THE PREVALENCE AND IMPACT OF SMARTPHONE ABUSE ON CHILDREN AND ADOLESCENTS

Children and adolescents are at particularly high risk of smartphone abuse and its negative consequences due to the prevalence of smartphone use and its impact on their developmental stages. According to a study conducted by Common Sense Media in 2019, 53% of children aged 8 to 12 owned a smartphone, and by the time they reached adolescence, this percentage increased to a staggering 84%. This prevalence can be attributed to several factors, including the affordability and accessibility of smartphones, peer pressure, and the desire to stay connected with friends and social networks. The impact of smartphone abuse on this age group can be far-reaching and detrimental to their physical, cognitive, and social well-being.

One of the significant concerns associated with smartphone abuse among children and adolescents is the negative impact it has on their physical health. Excessive smartphone use is often accompanied by a sedentary and inactive lifestyle, leading to a range of health problems such as obesity, musculoskeletal disorders, and sleep disturbances. The sedentary nature of smartphone use often displaces physical activities and outdoor play, resulting in reduced physical fitness and increased risks of chronic diseases. Excessive smartphone use, particularly during nighttime, disrupts sleep patterns and quality, leading to sleep deprivation and fatigue, which can negatively affect their academic performance and overall well-being. It is crucial to raise awareness among parents, educators, and healthcare professionals about the potential physical health consequences of smartphone abuse and encourage the adoption of strategies to promote a balanced and active lifestyle.

In addition to physical health concerns, smartphone abuse also has detrimental effects on children and adolescents' cognitive development. Excessive use of smartphones can impair attention and concentration, hinder memory and learning processes, and negatively affect academic achievements. The constant multi-tasking and distractions associated with smartphone use, such as push notifications, social media updates, and instant messaging, can fragment attention and impede deep learning. This fragmentation can lead to decreased productivity, decreased ability to focus and retain information, and Decreased academic success. Studies have shown that excessive smartphone use can lead to addictive behaviors and addiction-related brain changes, similar to substance abuse disorders. These cognitive impairments and addiction-like behaviors highlight the urgent need to implement strategies to promote healthy smartphone habits and ensure a conducive learning environment for children and adolescents. Another crucial aspect affected by smartphone abuse is children and adolescents' social development and interpersonal relationships. Excessive smartphone use can lead to social isolation, reduced face-to-face interactions, and impaired social skills. Studies have shown that heavy smartphone users tend to have smaller social networks, lower self-esteem, and higher levels of loneliness and depression. The constant comparison to others' online lives and the pressure to maintain an online persona can negatively impact self-esteem and contribute to feelings of inadequacy and anxiety. Excessive smartphone use can hinder the development of essential social skills, such as empathy, communication, and conflict resolution, as these skills are best acquired through face-to-face interactions. Consequently, it is vital to encourage children and adolescents to cultivate healthy offline relationships and participate in social activities that promote interpersonal connections. To combat smartphone abuse among children and adolescents, various strategies can be implemented, involving parents, educators, and policymakers. Firstly, parental involvement is crucial in setting boundaries and ensuring responsible smartphone use. Parents can establish clear rules and guidelines regarding smartphone usage, such as limiting screen time, implementing device-free zones, and monitoring their children's online activities. Regular communication and open dialogue about the potential risks of smartphone abuse can help foster a healthy relationship with technology and promote responsible digital citizenship. Secondly, educators and schools play a vital role in promoting digital literacy and responsible smartphone use. Integrating digital literacy programs into the curriculum and providing guidance on how to critically evaluate information, manage online privacy, and maintain a healthy balance between screen time and other activities can help equip children and adolescents with the necessary skills to navigate the digital world responsibly. Policymakers should address the issue of smartphone abuse through legislation and regulations. This can include implementing age restrictions for smartphone ownership, enforcing stricter guidelines for the marketing of smartphones targeted at children, and supporting public awareness campaigns that educate parents and children about the potential risks and consequences of smartphone abuse.

The prevalence and impact of smartphone abuse among children and adolescents are significant concerns that require immediate attention. The physical, cognitive, and social consequences associated with excessive smartphone use highlight the urgent need for strategies to combat this issue. By actively involving parents, educators, and policymakers in educating and guiding children and adolescents towards responsible smartphone use, we can promote a healthy and balanced relationship with technology and ensure their overall well-being and future success.

IMPORTANCE OF ADDRESSING SMARTPHONE ADDICTION IN THIS POPULATION

The importance of addressing smartphone addiction in the child and adolescent population cannot be overstated. As mentioned earlier, children and adolescents are particularly vulnerable to the negative impacts of excessive smartphone use due to their still-developing brains. Research has shown that excessive smartphone use can contribute to a range of physical and mental health issues in this age group. For instance, studies have indicated that excessive smartphone use can lead to poor sleep quality, which has been linked to various health problems such as obesity, diabetes, and mood disorders. The excessive use of smartphones has been found to negatively impact academic performance, with students who spend more time on their phones experiencing lower grades and reduced attention in class. This is particularly concerning as education is a crucial aspect of a child's development and future success. Addressing smartphone addiction in this population is therefore vital in order to mitigate these negative health and academic outcomes. Excessive smartphone use has been found to contribute to social and emotional difficulties among children and adolescents. Many young individuals are becoming increasingly reliant on smartphones for social interaction, leading to a decline in face-to-face communication skills and an increased risk of social isolation. Exposure to certain content on smartphones, such as cyberbullying or explicit material, can have detrimental effects on a child's mental well-being. By addressing smartphone addiction in this population, we can help children and adolescents develop healthier social interactions and strengthen their emotional well-being. The impact of excessive smartphone use extends beyond the individual and can have negative effects on families and relationships. Research has indicated that excessive smartphone use can lead to decreased parent-child interactions, as well as marital conflicts related to device use. This is particularly concerning given the importance of strong family relationships in a child's development. By addressing smartphone addiction in this population, we can help families establish healthier boundaries and enhance their overall well-being. The societal impact of smartphone addiction in children and adolescents should not be overlooked. Excessive smartphone use can contribute to a lack of physical activity, as children and adolescents spend more time on their devices and less time engaging in physical exercise. This can have long-term health consequences, including an increased risk of obesity and related chronic diseases. Excessive smartphone use can lead to negative behaviors such as cyberbullying and online harassment, which can have a detrimental impact on the social fabric of communities. By addressing smartphone addiction in this population, we can mitigate these societal consequences and promote healthier and more respectful online interactions. Addressing smartphone addiction in the child and adolescent population is of utmost importance. The negative consequences of excessive smartphone use on physical and mental health, academic performance, social and emotional well-being, family relationships, and societal interactions cannot be ignored. By implementing strategies to combat smartphone abuse in this population, such as education, setting boundaries, and promoting alternative activities, we can help mitigate these negative outcomes and foster healthier and more balanced smartphone usage. It is our responsibility as adults and educators to provide the necessary guidance and support to children and adolescents in navigating the digital world, ensuring their overall well-being and future success. Another effective strategy to combat smartphone abuse in children and adolescents is to create a supportive and open environment for communication. Parents should strive to establish a dialogue with their children about the dangers and consequences of excessive smartphone use. By maintaining an open line of communication, parents can better understand their children's concerns and pressures and provide guidance accordingly. This can also serve as an opportunity to educate children about responsible smartphone use and online safety. Parents should encourage their children to ask questions and express any concerns they may have about smartphone usage. By doing so, parents can address their children's fears and worries, thereby fostering a sense of trust and understanding within the family. Parents should also set clear boundaries and rules regarding smartphone usage. By establishing limits on screen time and defining specific situations when smartphone use is appropriate, parents can help their children develop healthier habits. Implementing a "no phone at the dinner table" policy or designating specific hours of the day as technology-free time can promote more face-to-face interactions and reduce dependency on smartphones. Parents should lead by example and demonstrate responsible smartphone use themselves. Children often model their behavior after their parents, so if parents are constantly glued to their phones, their children are more likely to do the same. Parents should be mindful of their own smartphone use and make a conscious effort to limit their screen time as well.

Parents should consider alternative activities or hobbies to engage their children in, such as sports, arts, or outdoor activities. By encouraging children to explore different interests and participate in various activities, parents can help divert their attention away from excessive smartphone use and foster healthy social interactions. Engaging in these activities together as a family can strengthen the bond between parents and children and provide a valuable opportunity for quality time spent together. Addressing the issue of smartphone abuse in children and adolescents requires a multi-faceted approach. It is crucial for parents, educators, and policymakers to collaborate and implement strategies to mitigate the negative effects of excessive smartphone use. By raising awareness about the potential dangers and consequences of smartphone abuse, providing education about responsible smartphone use, and creating a supportive and open environment for communication, we can combat this growing problem and ensure the healthy development of our children and adolescents.

II. THE CAUSES AND RISK FACTORS OF SMARTPHONE ABUSE IN CHILDREN AND ADOLESCENTS

In addition to emotional and psychological factors, there are several environmental and social risk factors that contribute to smartphone abuse in children and adolescents. Firstly, the increasing availability and affordability of smartphones have made them easily accessible to younger age groups. As a result, children and adolescents are more likely to own a smartphone and therefore be exposed to its potential addictive qualities. The widespread use of smartphones by parents and peers normalizes their presence in everyday life, further reinforcing the belief that constant smartphone use is acceptable and even expected.

The influence of social media and online platforms also plays a significant role in smartphone abuse among children and adolescents. Social media platforms provide an avenue for constant connectivity and validation, which can be particularly enticing to this vulnerable age group. The desire for social acceptance and the fear of missing out on social events or trends often drive excessive smartphone use. This can lead to a vicious cycle of seeking validation and approval through virtual interactions, resulting in a further detachment from the real world. The pressure to conform to societal norms and display an idealized version of oneself on social media further exacerbate the reliance on smartphones for self-esteem and identity validation.

The emergence of online gaming and gambling also contributes to smartphone abuse in children and adolescents. The gaming industry has capitalized on the addictive nature of video games and integrated them into the smartphone experience. Online gaming provides immediate gratification and a sense of achievement, leading individuals to spend extensive periods engrossed in their virtual worlds. The advent of gambling apps and online betting platforms has further magnified the risks associated with smartphone abuse. The easy accessibility and anonymity provided by these platforms make it increasingly challenging for children and adolescents to resist the lure of gambling and engage in responsible smartphone use.

Peer influence is another significant risk factor for smartphone abuse in this age group. Adolescents often feel compelled to conform to peer behaviors and expectations, including smartphone usage patterns. The fear of being left out or being perceived as different may drive them to constantly check their smartphones and engage in excessive screen time. Peer pressure can also manifest in the form of online bullying and cyberbullying, which further intensifies the need for constant digital connections. This not only increases the likelihood of smartphone abuse but also negatively impacts their emotional well-being and mental health. Parental behavior and family dynamics contribute to smartphone abuse in children and adolescents. The use of smartphones as a means of distraction and pacification by parents can inadvertently model unhealthy smartphone use. When parents prioritize their own smartphone use over meaningful interactions with their children, it sends a message that excessive screen time is acceptable. Parents who are overly permissive or fail to set boundaries regarding smartphone use create an enabling environment for smartphone abuse. Children and adolescents without clear guidelines or supervision are more likely to succumb to the addictive qualities of smartphones.

Societal pressure to excel academically and professionally also contributes to smartphone abuse in this age group. With smartphones providing easy access to information and resources, children and adolescents may feel compelled to constantly engage with their devices to stay ahead in their studies or extracurricular activities. The fear of missing out or falling behind academically further intensifies their reliance on smartphones, causing a detrimental impact on their overall well-being and academic performance.

Smartphone abuse in children and adolescents is a multi-dimensional issue influenced by various causes and risk factors. Environmental and social factors, such as the easy accessibility of smartphones, the influence of social media and online platforms, as well as peer influence, contribute to the addictive nature of smartphones. Parental behavior and societal pressures also play a significant role in facilitating smartphone abuse. Understanding these causes and risk factors is crucial for developing effective strategies to combat smartphone abuse in this vulnerable population. It requires a comprehensive approach involving parents, educators, healthcare professionals, and policymakers to promote responsible smartphone use and mitigate the potential harms associated with excessive screen time.

EASY ACCESSIBILITY AND AVAILABILITY OF SMARTPHONES

In addition to contributing to the high levels of smartphone use among children and adolescents, the easy accessibility and availability of these devices also pose a series of challenges in terms of promoting healthier screen habits. Smartphones have become a ubiquitous part of our society, with individuals of all ages relying on them for various purposes. This easy accessibility can be detrimental, particularly when it comes to children and adolescents who are at a crucial stage of development. The widespread availability of smartphones means that they are constantly within arm's reach, making it easy for young individuals to turn to these devices whenever they feel bored, anxious, or simply in need of stimulation. This instant gratification can create a dependency on smartphones, leading to an increase in screen time that negatively impacts various aspects of their lives, including academics, physical health, and social interactions. The availability of smartphones also exposes children and adolescents to potential dangers and harmful content. With an internet connection at their fingertips, young individuals can access inappropriate websites, interact with strangers, or fall victim to cyberbullying. This constant exposure to potentially harmful situations can have a profound impact on their mental and emotional well-being. It is imperative for parents, educators, and society at large to address the issue of easy accessibility and availability of smartphones and find strategies to manage and regulate their usage in order to promote healthier screen habits among children and adolescents.

INFLUENCE OF PEER PRESSURE AND SOCIAL MEDIA ON SMARTPHONE USE

In the realm of smartphone usage, peer pressure and social media play a significant role in influencing children and adolescents. Peer pressure, by definition, refers to the impact that individuals of the same age group have on one another. As digital natives, children and adolescents are highly susceptible to the influence of their peers when it comes to smartphone use. The desire to fit in and be accepted among their peers often results in the adoption of similar habits and behaviors. If a particular group of friends spends a significant amount of time on their smartphones, others are likely to follow suit in order to feel included. This peer pressure can be compounded by the pervasive nature of social media. Social media has become a prominent aspect of daily life for young individuals, with platforms like Instagram, Snapchat, and TikTok commanding their attention. These platforms not only serve as a means of communication but also showcase lifestyles, trends, and activities that can exert a tremendous influence on their users. The popularity of social media challenges children and adolescents to constantly stay connected, leading to an incessant need to check their smartphones for updates, likes, comments, and notifications. This need for instant gratification fuels the addictive nature of smartphone use and perpetuates a cycle of incessant scrolling, liking, and posting. Social media fosters a culture of comparison among young individuals. They are bombarded with images and posts that depict idealized versions of beauty, success, and happiness. In the pursuit of meeting these unrealistic standards, many children and adolescents find themselves spending excessive amounts of time on their smartphones, trying to curate an online presence that mirrors the perceived perfection of others. Consequently, they lose sight of their own self-worth and become increasingly dependent on their smartphones for validation and acceptance. This addiction to social media, driven by the fear of missing out or being left behind, creates a vicious cycle in which individuals become more entangled in their smartphones and less present in their real lives. The influence of peer pressure and social media on smartphone use can have detrimental effects on the well-being of children and adolescents. The excessive use of smartphones often leads to a sedentary lifestyle, contributing to physical health issues such as obesity and musculoskeletal problems. The constant exposure to social media's curated content can negatively impact mental health, fostering feelings of inadequacy, loneliness, and anxiety. The pressure to conform and be constantly connected can also hinder the development of real-life social skills, interpersonal relationships, and self-identity.

Addressing the influence of peer pressure and social media on smartphone use requires a multifaceted approach. First and foremost, it is crucial to educate children and adolescents about the potential negatives associated with excessive smartphone use. By fostering a sense of awareness, youngsters can develop a critical mindset that enables them to evaluate the reasons behind their smartphone usage and make informed decisions. Empowering individuals to understand the psychological and physical impacts of smartphone addiction helps them regain control over their own actions. Promoting a healthy balance between online and offline activities is paramount. Encouraging youngsters to engage in extracurricular activities, such as sports, hobbies, or social events, fosters the development of well-rounded individuals who are less reliant on their smartphones for entertainment and social validation. Creating designated screen-free times and spaces, such as family dinners or device-free bedrooms, further encourages individuals to disconnect from their smartphones and prioritize real-life interactions. It is essential for parents and educators to provide positive role modeling in relation to smartphone usage. By practicing what they preach, adults can demonstrate healthy smartphone habits, establishing a norm of responsible usage. Open dialogue and communication between parents, educators, and children is also crucial in understanding and guiding youngsters through the challenges of navigating a digitally saturated world. The influence of peer pressure and social media on smartphone use among children and adolescents cannot be underestimated. The need to fit in and seek acceptance, combined with the addictive nature of social media, drives individuals to spend excessive amounts of time on their smartphones. This phenomenon has detrimental effects on physical and mental health, interpersonal relationships, and self-identity. A comprehensive approach, encompassing education, awareness, balance, and positive role modeling, is necessary to combat smartphone abuse among young individuals. By empowering them to make conscious choices and providing a supportive environment, society can mitigate the negative consequences and foster healthier relationships with smartphones.

LACK OF PARENTAL GUIDANCE AND MONITORING

Lack of parental guidance and monitoring is another significant factor contributing to smartphone abuse in children and adolescents. In today's fast-paced and busy world, parents often find themselves overwhelmed with various responsibilities, making it challenging to actively supervise their children's smartphone usage. This lack of parental guidance can have severe consequences for children's well-being and development. Research suggests that children who lack proper parental guidance are more prone to engaging in excessive smartphone use, as they do not have clear boundaries or limitations set by their parents. Without proper supervision, children may not fully understand the potential risks associated with excessive smartphone use, such as cyberbullying, online harassment, and exposure to inappropriate content. In addition, the absence of parental monitoring may lead to a lack of healthy digital behaviors, such as time management, self-regulation, and responsible online communication.

The lack of parental guidance and monitoring can hinder children's overall development and academic performance. Excessive smartphone use has been linked to poor sleep patterns, reduced physical activity, and decreased social interactions, all of which can impact children's cognitive and social development. Studies have shown that children who spend more time on smartphones tend to have lower academic achievements, as their attention span and ability to concentrate are compromised. Without proper guidance, children may prioritize their virtual lives over their real-world responsibilities, leading to neglect of schoolwork, extracurricular activities, and interpersonal relationships. The absence of parental supervision also allows children to access and engage in age-inappropriate content and activities. Research suggests that children are more likely to stumble upon harmful or inappropriate content online without proper parental monitoring. This includes exposure to violent videos, explicit images, and adult-oriented websites. The lack of parental guidance can leave children vulnerable to online predators and groomers, who may take advantage of their innocence and naivety.

Without parental monitoring, children may unknowingly share personal information, engage in risky conversations, and fall victim to various forms of online exploitation.

The lack of parental guidance and monitoring can contribute to the development of unhealthy smartphone habits and addiction. Parents play a vital role in modeling responsible technology use and promoting healthy screen-time habits. When children do not receive proper guidance, they may become overly attached to their smartphones, relying on them for emotional comfort, validation, and constant entertainment. This dependency can lead to neglect of real-world activities, such as physical exercise, hobbies, and face-to-face social interactions. Children may also struggle to cope with boredom and solitude without their smartphones, as they have not been taught alternative ways to occupy their time and engage with the world around them.

To combat the lack of parental guidance and monitoring, various strategies can be implemented. Firstly, parents should strive to establish clear and consistent rules regarding smartphone use. Setting limits on screen time and establishing technology-free zones, such as the dinner table or bedrooms, can help create a healthy balance between offline and online activities. It is also important for parents to communicate openly with their children about the potential risks and consequences associated with excessive smartphone use. Discussing topics such as cyberbullying, online privacy, and responsible digital citizenship can help children understand the importance of using smartphones responsibly. In addition, parents should actively participate in their children's digital lives by monitoring their online activities and engaging in regular conversations about their smartphone use. This can be achieved through the use of parental control software, which allows parents to restrict access to certain websites, monitor text messages and social media activity, and set time limits on smartphone use. By taking an active interest in their children's online experiences, parents can better assess their children's behavior, ensure their safety, and provide guidance when necessary. Parents should aim to be positive role models for their children in terms of technology use. Demonstrating healthy phone habits, such as limiting their own screen time, being fully present during family activities, and prioritizing face-to-face interactions, can teach children the importance of balance and moderation. Parents should encourage and facilitate alternative activities that promote mental and physical well-being, such as outdoor play, reading, arts and crafts, and engaging in hobbies.

The lack of parental guidance and monitoring is a significant contributing factor to smartphone abuse in children and adolescents. Without proper supervision, children may engage in excessive smartphone use, exposing themselves to various risks and hindering their overall development. By implementing strategies such as setting clear rules, actively monitoring online activities, and modeling responsible screen-time habits, parents can effectively combat smartphone abuse and help their children develop healthier technology habits. It is crucial for parents to prioritize their children's well-being and actively participate in their digital lives to ensure a balanced and safe use of smartphones.

PSYCHOLOGICAL AND EMOTIONAL FACTORS CONTRIBUTING TO SMARTPHONE ADDICTION

While external factors such as easy accessibility and the constant connectivity offered by smartphones play a significant role in the development of smartphone addiction, it is important to acknowledge the psychological and emotional factors that contribute to this phenomenon. One psychological factor is the concept of escapism. For many individuals, smartphones provide an escape from the stresses and pressures of reality. Whether it is through engaging in mindless scrolling, playing addictive games, or indulging in social media, smartphones offer a temporary reprieve from the challenges of everyday life. This escape can be particularly enticing for individuals who struggle with emotional distress or mental health issues, as smartphones provide a readily available means of distraction. The instant gratification provided by smartphones through likes, comments, and notifications can have a profound impact on an individual's emotional state. The constant need for validation and the fear of missing out (FOMO) can create a sense of urgency, leading individuals to continuously check their smartphones for updates. This emotional reliance on smartphones further reinforces the addictive behavior. Another psychological factor that contributes to smartphone addiction is the phenomenon of social comparison. With social media platforms allowing individuals to present a curated version of their lives, it is common for users to compare themselves to others. This constant comparison can lead to feelings of inadequacy and low self-esteem, as individuals may perceive their own lives as less glamorous or fulfilling compared to their peers. This psychological impact can create a cycle of seeking validation and affirmation through constant smartphone use, further exacerbating the addiction. It is important to note that this phenomenon is particularly prevalent among children and adolescents who are in the process of forming their identities and are highly susceptible to societal pressures.

The concept of fear of missing out (FOMO) also plays a significant role in smartphone addiction. The fear of missing out on social events, news, or experiences can drive individuals to be constantly attached to their smartphones, fearing that they will miss out on something important. This fear is augmented by the constant stream of updates and notifications that smartphones provide. Individuals may feel a sense of anxiety or restlessness if they are unable to access their smartphones, reinforcing the addictive behavior. This emotional reliance on smartphones can have detrimental effects on an individual's mental well-being, as it hinders the ability to be fully present in the moment and fosters a sense of dependency on external stimuli.

The psychological factor of self-regulation and impulse control plays a pivotal role in smartphone addiction. Many individuals struggle with self-regulation, finding it difficult to resist the urge to constantly check their smartphones or engage in excessive screen time. This lack of impulse control can be especially prevalent among children and young adolescents, who are still developing their abilities to self-regulate. The immediate rewards offered by smartphones, such as the release of dopamine when receiving a notification, can override the impulse control mechanisms, leading to compulsive and addictive behavior. Individuals may use smartphones as a coping mechanism for dealing with negative emotions or boredom, substituting real-life experiences with virtual ones. This reliance on smartphones to regulate one's emotions can lead to a cycle of addiction, as individuals become increasingly dependent on their devices to manage their emotional states. While external factors such as accessibility and connectivity contribute to smartphone addiction, it is important to recognize the psychological and emotional factors that play a significant role in the development and perpetuation of this phenomenon. The escapism provided by smartphones, the psychological impact of social comparison, the fear of missing out (FOMO), and the struggle with self-regulation and impulse control all contribute to the addictive nature of smartphones. Understanding these psychological and emotional factors is crucial in developing effective strategies to combat smartphone abuse in children and adolescents. By addressing these underlying factors, it is possible to promote healthier and more balanced relationships with smartphones, ultimately fostering a generation of individuals who can utilize technology in a way that enhances their lives rather than hindering them.

One strategy to combat smartphone abuse in children and adolescents is to promote healthy and balanced screen time. The American Academy of Pediatrics recommends that children aged 6 years and older limit their recreational screen time to no more than two hours per day (AAP, 2016). This includes all forms of electronic media, such as television, computers, and smartphones (AAP, 2016). Enforcing this recommendation can be challenging, as smartphones have become integral to modern life and provide access to a wide range of educational and recreational content. It is important to strike a balance between the benefits of smartphone use and the potential negative effects of excessive screen time. One effective way to promote healthy screen time is by setting clear rules and boundaries for smartphone use. Parents and caregivers should establish specific time limits for recreational screen time and communicate these limits to children and adolescents. This can be done by creating a daily schedule that includes dedicated periods for smartphone use, such as after completing homework or chores. Setting consistent and reasonable boundaries will help children and adolescents develop self-regulation skills and understand the importance of balancing screen time with other activities.

In addition to time limits, parents and caregivers can encourage children and adolescents to engage in alternative activities that do not involve smartphones. This can include participating in sports, hobbies, or spending time with friends and family. By providing opportunities for offline activities, children and adolescents are more likely to develop a well-rounded set of interests and skills, which can help reduce their dependence on smartphones. Engaging in physical activities and social interactions can contribute to improved mental health and overall well-being, as excessive screen time has been linked to increased rates of anxiety, depression, and sleep disturbances (Twenge, 2017). Another strategy to combat smartphone abuse is to foster open and honest communication with children and adolescents about their smartphone use. Parents and caregivers should initiate conversations about the risks and benefits of smartphone use, and discuss the potential consequences of excessive screen time. By providing education and raising awareness about the potential negative effects of smartphone abuse, children and adolescents can make informed decisions about their own screen time habits. Parents and caregivers should serve as role models by demonstrating healthy smartphone behaviors themselves. This includes limiting their own screen time and being fully present during family activities and conversations.

It is important to promote the development of digital literacy skills in children and adolescents. This can include teaching them how to use smartphones responsibly, distinguish between credible and unreliable sources of information, and protect their personal privacy and security online. By empowering children and adolescents with the necessary skills to navigate the digital world, they are less likely to become overwhelmed or addicted to smartphone use. Teaching critical thinking skills can help them become more discerning consumers of media content and reduce their vulnerability to online manipulation and misinformation.

Parents and caregivers can utilize technological tools and resources to monitor and manage children and adolescents' smartphone use. There are various apps and software programs available that enable parents to set restrictions on screen time, block inappropriate content, and track smartphone usage. It is important to strike a balance between monitoring smartphone use and respecting children and adolescents' privacy. Trust and open communication are crucial in fostering healthy relationships with technology. Parents and caregivers should emphasize the importance of responsible and ethical smartphone use, and encourage children and adolescents to develop self-discipline and accountability. Combating smartphone abuse in children and adolescents requires a multifaceted approach that involves setting clear rules and boundaries, promoting alternative activities, fostering open communication, developing digital literacy skills, and utilizing technological tools. By implementing these strategies, parents and caregivers can help children and adolescents develop healthy and balanced screen time habits, while also reaping the benefits of smartphone use. It is important to remember that the goal is not to eliminate smartphone use altogether, but rather to ensure that it is used responsibly and in moderation. With intentional and mindful parenting, children and adolescents can navigate the digital world while maintaining a healthy and balanced lifestyle.

III. THE CONSEQUENCES OF SMARTPHONE ABUSE IN CHILDREN AND ADOLESCENTS

The consequences of smartphone abuse in children and adolescents are far-reaching and have significant implications for their overall well-being and development. Firstly, excessive smartphone use has been found to negatively impact physical health. Studies have shown that increased screen time is associated with sedentary behaviors and a decline in physical activity levels among young individuals (Twenge, 2018). This is concerning as lack of physical activity can lead to various health issues such as obesity, cardiovascular problems, and musculoskeletal disorders. Smartphone abuse can also affect mental health and cognitive development in children and adolescents. The constant exposure to social media platforms and online interactions can contribute to increased feelings of anxiety, depression, and loneliness (Twenge, 2018). The pressure to constantly compare oneself to others and seek validation through likes and comments can significantly impact a young person's self-esteem and overall mental well-being. Excessive smartphone use can impair concentration and attention span, leading to poor academic performance and diminished cognitive abilities (Billieux et al., 2015). This is particularly concerning given that adolescence is a critical period for learning and brain development.

The consequences of smartphone abuse also extend to social and emotional development. Excessive screen time can interfere with the development of healthy social relationships and the acquisition of crucial social skills (Twenge, 2018). Spending excessive time on smartphones often replaces face-to-face interactions, hindering the development of empathy, communication skills, and the ability to interpret nonverbal cues. This can result in difficulties forming and maintaining relationships, leading to feelings of isolation and loneliness.

Smartphone abuse can disrupt sleep patterns and have a detrimental impact on sleep quality in children and adolescents. The blue light emitted by smartphones can suppress the production of melatonin, a hormone critical for regulating sleep-wake cycles, making it harder for young individuals to fall asleep and maintain a healthy sleep schedule (Cain & Gradisar, 2010). Chronic sleep deprivation can have numerous negative effects on physical and mental health, including impaired cognitive function, increased risk of mood disorders, and compromised immune system functioning. Another consequence of smartphone abuse in children and adolescents is the potential for exposure to inappropriate content, cyberbullying, and online predators. With unrestricted access to the internet, young individuals may inadvertently stumble upon explicit or violent material, which can have a lasting negative impact on their psychological well-being. In addition, the ability to communicate and interact with others online also puts them at risk of becoming victims of cyberbullying or being targeted by individuals with malicious intentions, such as online predators (Moreno et al., 2016). This can cause significant distress and trauma, ultimately leading to long-term psychological harm. Smartphone abuse can also have an economic impact on individuals and society as a whole. Excessive smartphone use can lead to decreased productivity and impaired performance in

academic or professional settings. This can result in missed opportunities and setbacks in educational or career
paths. The use of smartphones for entertainment and leisure activities can become addictive, leading to financial difficulties as individuals spend excessive amounts of money on apps, games, and subscription services (Billieux et al., 2015).

The consequences of smartphone abuse in children and adolescents span across physical, mental, social, and economic domains. Sedentary behavior, impaired mental health, disrupted sleep patterns, hindered social and emotional development, exposure to inappropriate content, and decreased productivity are just a few of the negative consequences associated with excessive smartphone use. It is crucial for parents, educators, and policymakers to recognize the gravity of this issue and implement strategies and interventions aimed at combating smartphone abuse in young individuals. By promoting healthy technology use habits and encouraging a balanced lifestyle, we can mitigate the adverse effects of smartphone addiction and safeguard the well-being and development of children and adolescents.

NEGATIVE EFFECTS ON PHYSICAL HEALTH AND WELL-BEING

Excessive smartphone use can have detrimental effects on physical health and overall well-being. One negative effect is the impact on sleep patterns and quality. Studies have shown that the blue light emitted by smartphones can interfere with the production of melatonin, a hormone that regulates sleep. This can lead to difficulties falling asleep and staying asleep, resulting in sleep disturbances and insomnia. Inadequate sleep not only affects a person's mood and cognitive function but also has significant implications for physical health. It increases the risk of developing chronic conditions such as obesity, diabetes, and cardiovascular diseases. Excessive smartphone use often leads to a sedentary lifestyle, reducing physical activity levels. Instead of engaging in outdoor activities or exercise, children and adolescents may spend hours sitting or lying down, engrossed in their smartphones. This lack of physical activity can contribute to weight gain and obesity, as well as to the development of musculoskeletal problems such as back and neck pain. In addition, prolonged smartphone use can strain the eyes, leading to symptoms such as dryness, irritation, and blurry vision, commonly known as computer vision syndrome. The constant focusing on the small screens and the increased use of near vision associated with smartphone use can lead to eye strain and increased risk of myopia progression in children and adolescents. These physical health issues not only have immediate consequences but can also have long-term effects, negatively impacting a person's quality of life and overall well-being. Excessive smartphone use can also negatively affect mental health. Research has shown a strong association between excessive screen time and increased symptoms of anxiety and depression in children and adolescents. The constant exposure to social media platforms and the virtual world can lead to feelings of loneliness, low self-esteem, and social isolation. The addictive nature of smartphones can result in excessive dopamine release in the brain, similar to that seen in substance abuse disorders. This can create a cycle of dependency, where individuals rely on their smartphones for a sense of pleasure or relief from negative emotions. The constant need for validation or fear of missing out (FOMO) drives individuals to excessively check their devices, leading to heightened anxiety and stress levels. These mental health issues can have significant consequences on overall well-being, affecting relationships, academic performance, and personal development. Excessive smartphone use can also have negative effects on social well-being. The excessive reliance on virtual communication can result in decreased face-to-face social interactions, leading to a decline in social skills and social connections. Many individuals, especially children and adolescents, prioritize virtual interactions over real-life relationships, leading to feelings of loneliness and isolation. The constant distraction of smartphones also interferes with the ability to fully engage in social situations, limiting the depth of conversations and meaningful interactions. Excessive screen time can also negatively impact family dynamics, as members may become disconnected and detached from each other. The exposure to cyberbullying and online harassment through social media platforms can further erode social well-being, causing significant emotional distress and social withdrawal.

Excessive smartphone use has numerous negative effects on physical health and overall well-being. From sleep disturbances to sedentary lifestyles and musculoskeletal problems, the physical health implications are significant and can have long-term consequences. In terms of mental health, excessive screen time has been linked to increased symptoms of anxiety and depression, as well as addictive behaviors. Social well-being is also negatively affected, with a decline in face-to-face interactions and social connections. It is crucial for parents, educators, and society as a whole to address this issue and implement strategies to combat smartphone abuse in children and adolescents, promoting a healthier and more balanced approach to technology use.

IMPACTS ON MENTAL HEALTH, INCLUDING INCREASED ANXIETY AND DEPRESSION

One of the most concerning consequences of smartphone abuse is the detrimental impact it can have on mental health, leading to increased levels of anxiety and depression among children and adolescents. The constant exposure to social media, online bullying, and the pressure to constantly compare oneself to others can all contribute to feelings of unease and inadequacy. A study conducted by Twenge et al. (2018) found a significant correlation between smartphone use and mental health issues, with adolescents who spent more time on their phones reporting higher levels of psychological distress. This suggests that excessive smartphone use may act as a catalyst for the development of anxiety and depression symptoms. The function of social media platforms as highlight reels of others' lives often fosters feelings of envy and self-doubt, further exacerbating these mental health issues. One reason why smartphone use can negatively impact mental health is the addictive nature of these devices. Smartphone addiction, also known as nomophobia, can lead to anxiety symptoms such as restlessness, irritability, and withdrawal when the phone is unavailable or not being used. The constant need to be connected and fear of missing out on social events or important information can create a heightened sense of anxiety among young individuals. The availability of social media platforms at any time can lead to sleep disturbances, as individuals often find themselves staying up late scrolling through their feeds. Sleep deprivation, in turn, can contribute to the development of anxiety and depressive symptoms. A study by Sampasa-Kanyinga and Lewis (2015) found that inadequate sleep, partly caused by excessive smartphone use, was associated with higher levels of depression and anxiety among adolescents. Cyberbullying has become a widespread issue among children and adolescents due to the increased access to online platforms. The anonymity provided by the internet makes it easier for bullies to target their victims without facing immediate consequences. Victims of cyberbullying often experience increased levels of stress, fear, and social isolation, which can lead to the development of anxiety and depression. A study conducted by Kowalski et al. (2014) found that cyber victims were more likely to report symptoms of depression and anxiety compared to those who had not experienced cyberbullying. This highlights the negative impact that smartphone use can have on mental well-being by exposing individuals to a new type of harassment that can extend beyond the confines of traditional bullying.

Another detrimental aspect of excessive smartphone use is the constant comparison to others that occurs on social media platforms. The curated nature of online profiles often leads individuals to portray an idealized version of their lives, showcasing only the positive aspects and achievements. This creates an unrealistic expectation of what life should be like, further perpetuating feelings of inadequacy and self-doubt. The constant exposure to these seemingly perfect lives can foster feelings of envy and fuel a cycle of negative self-comparison, leading to increased levels of anxiety and depression. A study conducted by Lee and Lee (2017) found that the more time adolescents spent on social media, the more they engaged in social comparison, which in turn predicted higher levels of depression and anxiety.

The continuous use of smartphones and exposure to idealized online lives can significantly contribute to the deterioration of mental health in young individuals.

The impacts of smartphone abuse on mental health, particularly increased anxiety and depression, are undeniable. The addictive nature of these devices, coupled with the constant access to social media platforms and exposure to cyberbullying, creates a toxic environment for the psychological well-being of children and adolescents. It is essential for parents, educators, and society as a whole to develop strategies to combat smartphone abuse and protect the mental health of young individuals. By promoting healthy boundaries, fostering open communication, and raising awareness about the potential consequences of excessive smartphone use, it is possible to mitigate the negative effects and cultivate a generation that is well-equipped to navigate the digital world while prioritizing their mental well-being.

DETRIMENTS TO ACADEMIC PERFORMANCE AND PRODUCTIVITY

Excessive smartphone use can have detrimental effects on academic performance and productivity. One of the main reasons for this is the distraction smartphones pose in educational settings. With a smartphone constantly at their fingertips, students may struggle to concentrate on their studies and become easily sidetracked by social media notifications and text messages. A study conducted by Junco and Cotten (2012) found that students who frequently used their smartphones during class had lower grades compared to those who refrained from such behavior. The constant interruptions from phone usage can disrupt the flow of learning and hinder the ability to retain information effectively.

Smartphone addiction can lead to a decline in the quality of work produced by students. Spending excessive amounts of time on smartphones can result in a lack of focus and attention to detail, leading to subpar performance on assignments and exams. Students may also become reliant on their smartphones for information instead of engaging in active learning and critical thinking. This over-reliance on technology can hinder the development of essential skills and the ability to think independently.

The excessive use of smartphones can have negative effects on sleep patterns, which, in turn, can further compromise academic performance. The blue light emitted by screens suppresses the production of melatonin, a hormone that regulates sleep. Numerous studies have shown that exposure to blue light before bedtime can disrupt sleep quality and quantity (Chang et al., 2015).

Lack of adequate sleep negatively impacts cognitive functioning, including attention, memory, and problem-solving abilities, all of which are crucial for academic success. Students who are sleep-deprived are likely to experience difficulty concentrating in class and may struggle to retain information during study sessions.

Another detrimental aspect of smartphone abuse on academic performance and productivity is the phenomenon known as "multitasking." Many students believe that they can effectively perform multiple tasks simultaneously, such as texting while studying, but research suggests otherwise. Contrary to popular belief, multitasking actually decreases productivity and efficiency. A study by Wang et al. (2012) found that individuals who engaged in multitasking took longer to complete tasks, made more errors, and had difficulty maintaining focus on each activity. Consequently, students who engage in smartphone multitasking are likely to experience diminished performance on academic assignments and exams, as their attention is divided between multiple tasks. Constant smartphone usage can contribute to heightened levels of stress and anxiety among students. The pressure to constantly update social media profiles and be available for instant communication can create a sense of urgency and unease. This constant need for connectivity can be overwhelming and lead to increased stress levels. Research by Elhai et al. (2018) found a positive correlation between excessive smartphone use and higher stress levels in college students. This added stress can impair students' ability to concentrate, absorb new information, and perform well academically.

The consequences of excessive smartphone use on academic performance and productivity are profound. It not only hinders concentration and focus but also leads to a decline in the quality of work produced by students. Lack of sleep, caused by prolonged smartphone use, further exacerbates these issues. Multitasking, often perceived as efficient, actually decreases productivity. The constant connectivity and pressure to engage in social media can create heightened levels of stress and anxiety among students. As the prevalence of smartphone abuse continues to rise among children and adolescents, it is imperative for parents, educators, and policymakers to implement strategies that address and combat this issue to ensure optimal academic outcomes and overall well-being.

SOCIAL AND INTERPERSONAL CONSEQUENCES: REDUCED FACE-TO-FACE COMMUNICATION SKILLS

Reduced face-to-face communication skills are among the social and interpersonal consequences of excessive smartphone use in children and adolescents. In an era dominated by screens and virtual interactions, many young individuals find it increasingly challenging to strike up conversations or engage in face-to-face interactions with others. The constantly available virtual world offered by smartphones can create a sense of comfort and security, allowing individuals to avoid the potential discomfort that can accompany social interactions. Consequently, the development of essential social skills, such as maintaining eye contact, interpreting nonverbal cues, and active listening, may be hindered. This deficit in face-to-face communication skills can have significant repercussions on various aspects of an individual's life. One of the most apparent impacts of reduced face-to-face communication skills is difficulty in establishing and maintaining meaningful relationships. Human connection relies heavily on nonverbal cues and subtle gestures, which are often absent in the digital realm. Without the ability to effectively interpret these cues, individuals may struggle to form close bonds with others, resulting in feelings of isolation and loneliness. This can be particularly detrimental during adolescence, a period marked by the formation of identity and the need for social validation. The pervasive use of smartphones can lead to an overreliance on virtual interactions and a neglect of the nuanced social connections that can only be established through face-to-face communication.

Reduced face-to-face communication skills can negatively impact academic performance. Classroom settings often necessitate students' active participation in discussions, group projects, and presentations. These activities require individuals to articulate their thoughts, comprehend complex ideas, and present them coherently. If students lack robust face-to-face communication skills, they may struggle to express themselves effectively, resulting in diminished academic engagement and performance. Reduced ability to engage in real-time discussions with peers and teachers can limit opportunities for collaboration and learning from different perspectives. Consequently, students may miss out on the benefits of critical thinking, problem-solving, and creativity that arise from face-to-face interactions.

The workplace is another domain affected by reduced face-to-face communication skills. Effective communication is a fundamental skill sought by employers, one that extends beyond mere technical expertise. Face-to-face interactions in the workplace enable individuals to build rapport, establish trust, and effectively communicate complex ideas. Individuals who lack these skills may face challenges in navigating the intricacies of professional relationships, hindering their career advancement. Reduced face-to-face communication skills can hinder networking opportunities, as establishing connections and building professional relationships often requires effective interpersonal skills. As the digital era continues to evolve, the imperative for individuals to possess strong face-to-face communication skills remains essential for professional success.

The consequences of reduced face-to-face communication skills extend beyond personal relationships and professional settings. They have the potential to impact mental health and emotional well-being. Face-to-face interactions offer a unique opportunity for emotional connection, empathy, and support, which virtual interactions may struggle to replicate. Without the ability to engage effectively in these interactions, individuals may experience a sense of disconnection and alienation. Lacking the skills to navigate social situations can lead to social anxiety and diminished self-confidence, further exacerbating feelings of isolation and loneliness. Consequently, individuals may retreat further into their virtual worlds, perpetuating a harmful cycle of reliance on screens and superficial connections.

Reduced face-to-face communication skills are a significant social and interpersonal consequence of smartphone addiction in children and adolescents. The ability to communicate effectively in person is crucial for the establishment of meaningful relationships, academic success, career advancement, and emotional well-being. As society becomes increasingly reliant on digital interactions, it is essential to recognize the importance of face-to-face communication skills and promote strategies to combat excessive smartphone use. By fostering an awareness of the potential consequences and providing individuals with opportunities for interpersonal connections, we can mitigate the negative impact of smartphone abuse and cultivate a generation capable of thriving in both virtual and real-world interactions.

Screen time has become a pervasive issue in the lives of children and adolescents, with smartphones serving as the primary source of this addiction. The consequences of excessive screen time are deeply concerning, as it not only affects their physical health but also hinders their cognitive and social development. While many parents and educators grapple with this issue, it is necessary to consider effective strategies to combat smartphone abuse in this vulnerable population. One proven strategy is establishing clear boundaries and rules regarding screen time and smartphone usage. By setting limits on the amount of time children and adolescents can spend on their smartphones, parents can help them develop healthy habits from an early age and avoid falling into the trap of screen addiction. For instance, parents may enforce restrictions on the number of hours spent on screens and implement designated screen-free zones in the house. A structured routine that includes specific times for activities such as physical exercise, studying, and social interaction can contribute to a more balanced lifestyle, reducing the allure of smartphone use.

In addition to setting boundaries, it is essential to educate children and adolescents about the risks associated with excessive screen time. Many young individuals may not fully comprehend the potential long-term consequences of their smartphone addiction. Educating them about the negative impact on physical health, such as the increased risk of obesity and sedentary lifestyle, can empower them to make informed choices regarding their screen usage. Highlighting the detrimental effects on mental health, such as poor self-esteem, depression, anxiety, and social isolation, can help them grasp the significance of reducing their screen time. By elucidating these risks, parents and educators can foster a sense of responsibility and motivation among children and adolescents to monitor and limit their smartphone usage. A further strategy to combat smartphone abuse is promoting alternative activities that can engage children and adolescents in a healthier manner. Encouraging physical activities, including sports, outdoor games, and exercise, not only reduces screen time but also has numerous physical and mental health benefits. Engaging in creative and artistic pursuits, such as painting, writing, or playing a musical instrument, can also divert their attention from screens while fostering self-expression and enhancing cognitive abilities. Developing interpersonal skills through activities like team sports, volunteering, or joining clubs can help them cultivate meaningful relationships, reducing their reliance on virtual interactions. To combat screen addiction, it is crucial to emphasize the importance of family time and quality interpersonal connections. Encouraging regular family activities, such as board games or outdoor outings, can create opportunities for bonding while minimizing screen use. Parents can also demonstrate healthy smartphone habits by limiting their own screen time and actively participating in face-to-face interactions with their children. By modeling responsible behavior, parents can instill values of balanced screen use and meaningful human connections. Implementing technology-use monitoring tools and parental control apps can provide additional support in combatting smartphone abuse. These tools allow parents to track and restrict their child's screen time, block specific apps or websites, and set limits on the use of smartphones. Such measures can help parents establish a balance between technological exposure and other vital aspects of their child's life. Nonetheless, the use of these tools should be accompanied by open communication and trust to ensure that children and adolescents understand the rationale behind these restrictions.

Collaboration between schools, parents, and educators is crucial in addressing smartphone addiction successfully. Schools can incorporate digital literacy and wellness programs into the curriculum, educating students about the balanced use of technology and its impact on their well-being. Teachers can play an active role by encouraging offline activities and promoting face-to-face interactions in the classroom. Schools can organize seminars and workshops for parents, providing them with the necessary knowledge and strategies to guide their children towards a healthy relationship with screens.

Combating smartphone abuse in children and adolescents requires a multi-faceted approach that involves setting clear boundaries, educating about the risks, promoting alternative activities, emphasizing interpersonal connections, utilizing monitoring tools, and fostering collaboration between parents and educators. By implementing these strategies, society can help young individuals develop a healthy relationship with technology, leading to improved physical and mental well-being, enhanced cognitive abilities, and stronger interpersonal skills. It is essential to recognize that reducing smartphone addiction is a collective effort that requires the dedication and involvement of parents, educators, and policymakers to safeguard the future generations from the perils of excessive screen time.

IV. STRATEGIES FOR PARENTS TO COMBAT SMARTPHONE ABUSE IN CHILDREN AND ADOLESCENTS

One important strategy for parents to combat smartphone abuse in children and adolescents is setting clear and consistent boundaries. By establishing specific rules and expectations regarding smartphone use, parents can provide structure and guidance for their children. For example, parents may limit the amount of time their child can spend on the smartphone each day or restrict its usage to certain hours. This can help prevent excessive smartphone use and create a healthy balance between screen time and other activities. Parents should consistently enforce these rules and consequences for any violations, which can help children understand the importance of responsible and controlled smartphone use. By setting boundaries, parents can not only promote healthier habits but also foster self-discipline and self-regulation skills in their children. Parents can actively engage in monitoring their child's smartphone use to ensure compliance with the established rules. This can be done through various methods, such as reviewing their child's phone activity regularly or using parental control applications to track screen time and limit access to inappropriate content. By staying vigilant and involved, parents can effectively combat smartphone abuse and prevent their children from engaging in potentially harmful behaviors. It is crucial for parents to strike a balance between monitoring and respecting their child's privacy to maintain trust and open communication. Parents should also lead by example and demonstrate healthy smartphone behavior themselves. Children often learn from observing their parents' actions, so if parents consistently model responsible smartphone use, their children are more likely to follow suit. Parents can prioritize face-to-face interactions, engage in outdoor activities, and establish smartphone-free zones to emphasize the importance of real-world connections over virtual ones. By being mindful of their own smartphone usage, parents can instill good habits and values in their children, ultimately helping them develop a healthier relationship with technology.

ESTABLISHING AND ENFORCING SCREEN TIME LIMITS

In order to address the issue of smartphone abuse among children and adolescents, establishing and enforcing screen time limits is crucial. Research has consistently shown that excessive screen time has negative effects on physical and mental health, academic performance, and social skills. It is imperative for parents, schools, and policymakers to work together to set appropriate limits on the amount of time that children and adolescents can spend on their devices. To facilitate this, parents should lead by example and establish clear rules and expectations regarding screen time. They can set specific time intervals during which screen time is allowed, such as limiting it to a certain number of hours per day or only allowing screen time after completing homework or chores. Parents should encourage their children to engage in alternative activities that are not device-dependent, such as outdoor play, reading, or pursuing hobbies. Schools also play a vital role in managing screen time by incorporating it into their curriculum. They can implement policies that restrict or regulate device usage during school hours, ensuring that students have limited access to their smartphones and other gadgets. By doing so, schools can encourage students to focus on their studies and develop better concentration and attention skills. It is essential for schools to educate both students and parents about the potential dangers and consequences of excessive screen time. It is equally important for policy-makers to step in and take a proactive approach to address this issue. They can develop and enforce regulations that ensure technology companies provide tools and features to help parents and users limit screen time on devices. These tools can include features like app timers, restricted modes, and automatic reminders. Policy-makers should invest in campaigns that raise awareness about responsible screen time usage and promote digital literacy among children and adolescents. By taking a multi-faceted approach involving parents, schools, and policy-makers, we can effectively establish and enforce screen time limits and combat smartphone abuse among younger generations. It is crucial to remember that simply setting limits is not enough. Alongside these rules, it is imperative to create a nurturing environment where children and adolescents can develop healthier relationships with technology. This environment includes open and honest conversations about the potential risks and benefits of technology, as well as fostering a supportive community that encourages face-to-face connections. Parents and caregivers must strive to maintain open lines of communication with their children and be willing to understand their experiences and concerns regarding technology. They should regularly review and update their rules and boundaries regarding screen time to adapt to the evolving technology landscape. Schools should also prioritize teaching digital literacy skills that will equip students with the ability to navigate the digital world responsibly. By integrating digital citizenship and media literacy education into their curriculum, schools can empower students with the knowledge and skills they need to make informed and responsible decisions about their technology use. Policy-makers need to engage in ongoing research on the impacts of screen time and smartphone abuse to inform future policy decisions. By staying up-to-date with the latest findings, policy-makers can create evidence-based guidelines that can effectively address the issue. Establishing and enforcing screen time limits is a crucial step in combating smartphone abuse in children and adolescents. Parents, schools, and policy-makers have a shared responsibility in creating an environment that promotes responsible technology use. By leading by example, establishing clear rules, and fostering open communication, parents can help their children develop healthier relationships with technology. Schools should implement policies that limit device usage during school hours and educate students about responsible screen time usage. Policy-makers should develop regulations and awareness campaigns to promote responsible technology use and support parents and schools in their efforts. Together, by adhering to screen time limits and creating a nurturing environment, we can mitigate the harmful effects of excessive screen time and empower future generations to use technology in a responsible and balanced manner.

ENCOURAGING AND FACILITATING ALTERNATIVE ACTIVITIES AND HOBBIES

In order to combat smartphone abuse in children and adolescents, it is essential to encourage and facilitate alternative activities and hobbies. By providing young individuals with enjoyable and fulfilling alternatives to screen time, we can redirect their attention and engagement towards more meaningful and productive pursuits. One effective strategy is to engage them in physical activities and outdoor sports. Encouraging regular exercise not only promotes physical well-being but also helps in reducing screen time. Organized sports teams or community programs that offer opportunities for young people to participate in team sports and outdoor activities can be highly beneficial. Such activities not only help in fostering social interaction but also enhance physical fitness and overall health.

Promoting creative and artistic hobbies can be a great way to divert attention from excessive smartphone use. Activities such as painting, drawing, playing a musical instrument, or writing can provide an outlet for self-expression and allow children and adolescents to explore their creativity. Artistic endeavors have been shown to boost cognitive skills, improve self-esteem, and foster personal growth. To facilitate these activities, parents and educators can provide access to art supplies, musical instruments, or creative writing workshops. Creating an environment that supports and encourages these hobbies can significantly reduce the reliance on smartphones for entertainment.

Engaging in intellectual and educational pursuits can be an

effective method to combat smartphone addiction. Encouraging reading habits by providing access to books and creating designated reading spaces can help develop a love for literature. Reading not only expands vocabulary and improves critical thinking skills but also encourages imagination and creativity. Educational games and puzzles can also be incorporated to make learning entertaining and engaging. By promoting a culture of learning and intellectual curiosity, young individuals are more likely to find fulfillment in educational activities rather than mindlessly scrolling through smartphones.

Encouraging participation in community service and volunteering is another strategy that can divert attention away from smartphones. Engaging in meaningful initiatives allows children and adolescents to develop empathy, compassion, and a sense of social responsibility. By contributing to the well-being of others, young individuals learn valuable life skills, build their character, and gain a sense of purpose.

Parents, schools, and community organizations can collaborate to provide opportunities for young people to volunteer in local charities, help the elderly, or participate in environmental conservation efforts. By actively involving themselves in community service, young individuals not only reduce their dependence on smartphones but also become valued members of society.

Promoting healthy social interactions is crucial in combating smartphone abuse. Encouraging face-to-face communication and fostering interpersonal connections can help reduce the need for constant virtual interactions. Parents and educators can facilitate social gatherings, organize group activities, and promote team-based projects that require collaboration and cooperation. By fostering positive social relationships, young individuals develop important social skills, build self-confidence, and form lasting friendships. It is also important to educate young people about the potential dangers of excessive smartphone use and the importance of setting healthy boundaries in their online and offline interactions. Combating smartphone abuse in children and adolescents requires a multi-faceted approach that addresses the underlying causes and provides strategies for change. Encouraging and facilitating alternative activities and hobbies play a crucial role in redirecting attention from screens to more fulfilling pursuits. By engaging young individuals in physical activities, artistic hobbies, intellectual pursuits, and community service, we provide them with opportunities for personal growth, social interaction, and a sense of purpose. Parents, educators, and community organizations must work together to create an environment that supports and encourages these alternative activities. Together, we can help young individuals break free from the shackles of smartphone addiction and lead balanced and fulfilling lives.

OPEN LINES OF COMMUNICATION AND ESTABLISHING TRUST WITH CHILDREN

Open lines of communication and establishing trust with children are crucial in addressing smartphone abuse. Parents should create an environment where children feel comfortable discussing their digital use and any concerns they may have. Regular conversations should take place to help children understand the potential negative consequences of excessive smartphone use and to educate them about responsible usage. By actively listening to their children's experiences and opinions, parents can gain valuable insights into their child's mindset and the specific factors driving their smartphone addiction. Parents should encourage open and honest dialogue about the dangers of smartphone abuse, such as cyberbullying, online predators, and the impact on mental health. By creating a non-judgmental atmosphere, parents can ensure that their children feel safe seeking help and guidance when needed. Trust is built when parents display understanding, empathy, and support rather than resorting to strict monitoring and control.

SETTING A GOOD EXAMPLE BY LIMITING PERSONAL SMARTPHONE USE

Can be a highly effective strategy in combatting smartphone abuse in children and adolescents. Children often model their behavior after their parents or caregivers, so if these individuals are constantly glued to their phones, it is likely that children will follow suit. It is crucial for adults to demonstrate responsible smartphone use and set clear boundaries for themselves. By limiting their own personal smartphone use, adults can teach children the importance of balance and moderation when it comes to technology. This can be achieved by designating specific times during the day when devices are off-limits, such as during family meals or certain evening hours. Adults can establish smartphone-free zones in specific areas of the house, such as bedrooms or the dining table, to help create a healthy separation between technology and personal life. By adhering to these boundaries themselves, adults can show children the importance of disconnecting from their devices and engaging in face-to-face interactions. Adults can engage in activities that do not involve screen time, such as reading a book or engaging in outdoor activities, which can serve as a tangible example for children to follow. By observing these behaviors, children can learn to prioritize real-life experiences over digital ones and develop a healthier relationship with technology. It is important to note that setting a good example in limiting personal smartphone use is not just limited to parents and caregivers – it extends to all influential adults in a child's life, such as teachers and mentors. These individuals should also strive to establish boundaries around their own smartphone use, both in and outside the classroom, and encourage students to do the same. By demonstrating that smartphone use should be purposeful and intentional, educators can help students understand the importance of minimizing distractions and staying focused on the tasks at hand. Educators can incorporate activities and assignments that do not involve smartphones or other screens, providing students with alternative ways to learn and engage in the world around them. Adults can engage children and adolescents in conversations about the consequences of excessive smartphone use, emphasizing the negative impact it can have on their mental health, social skills, and academic performance. By sharing personal experiences or anecdotes, adults can illustrate the potential pitfalls of over-reliance on smartphones and underscore the value of balance and moderation. Setting a good example by limiting personal smartphone use is an essential strategy in combating smartphone abuse in children and adolescents. By demonstrating responsible technology use, adults can teach children the importance of balance and the ability to disconnect from their devices.

Adults can engage in screen-free activities and establish smartphone-free zones, creating a healthy separation between technology and personal life. Teachers and other influential adults can also contribute by modeling responsible smartphone use and incorporating non-screen activities into the curriculum. By fostering conversations about the consequences of excessive smartphone use, adults can help children and adolescents develop a healthier relationship with technology and prioritize real-life experiences. By taking these steps, adults can play a crucial role in combatting smartphone abuse in children and adolescents and promoting healthy digital habits.

There are several strategies that can be implemented to combat smartphone abuse in children and adolescents. One of the most effective strategies is setting limits and boundaries around smartphone use. Parents can establish specific rules and guidelines for phone usage, such as limiting the amount of time spent on the device or designating certain hours of the day as "phone-free time". By setting clear boundaries, parents can help children and adolescents develop healthier habits and promote a balanced lifestyle. Another strategy to combat smartphone abuse is fostering open communication and dialogue about the potential risks and consequences associated with excessive phone use. Parents should engage in regular conversations with their children about the importance of moderation and address concerns about the negative impact of smartphone addiction. By discussing these issues openly, parents can help children and adolescents understand the potential harms and make informed decisions about their phone use. In addition to establishing limits and promoting open communication, it is essential for parents to model healthy smartphone behavior themselves. Children and adolescents often mimic the behavior of their parents, so if parents are constantly on their phones, it sends the message that excessive phone use is acceptable. Parents should be mindful of their own phone usage and strive to be good role models for their children. They can demonstrate healthy boundaries by putting their phones away during family meals, engaging in activities that do not involve screens, and prioritizing face-to-face interactions over virtual ones. It is important to educate children and adolescents about the potential dangers of excessive smartphone use. Parents can provide information about the negative effects of screen addiction on physical and mental health, social relationships, and academic performance. By raising awareness about these risks, parents can empower children and adolescents to make responsible choices regarding their phone usage. Implementing technology breaks and encouraging alternative activities can be an effective strategy to combat smartphone abuse. Parents can encourage their children to participate in physical activities, hobbies, and social interactions that do not involve screens. They can also establish designated technology-free zones in the house, such as bedrooms or study areas. By creating opportunities for offline activities, parents can help children and adolescents develop a healthier balance between screen time and other aspects of their lives.

In addition to these strategies, parents can utilize parental control tools and apps to monitor and limit their children's smartphone use. These tools allow parents to track how much time their children spend on their phones, block certain apps or websites, and set time limits for screen time. By using these tools, parents can have more control over their children's phone usage and protect them from the negative consequences of excessive screen time. It is important for parents to cultivate a supportive and understanding environment for their children as they navigate the challenges of smartphone use. Instead of blaming or shaming children for their excessive phone use, parents should approach the issue with empathy and a willingness to help. They can provide resources, such as counseling or support groups, for children and adolescents who are struggling with screen addiction. By offering support and understanding, parents can create a safe space for their children to address and overcome their smartphone abuse. Combating smartphone abuse in children and adolescents requires a multi-faceted approach. By setting limits and boundaries, fostering open communication, modeling healthy behavior, educating about the risks, encouraging alternative activities, utilizing parental control tools, and creating a supportive environment, parents can effectively reduce the negative impact of excessive phone use. It is essential for parents to take an active role in helping their children develop healthy habits and promote a balanced lifestyle in the digital age.

V. SCHOOL-BASED INTERVENTIONS TO ADDRESS SMARTPHONE ABUSE

School-based interventions to address smartphone abuse have proven to be effective in reducing excessive smartphone use among children and adolescents. One such intervention is the implementation of educational programs that provide students with information about the negative consequences of smartphone abuse. These programs aim to increase awareness among students about the potential harms of excessive smartphone use, such as negative impacts on mental health, social relationships, and academic performance. By educating students about these risks, school-based interventions empower them to make informed choices about their smartphone usage and develop healthier relationships with technology.

Another effective school-based intervention is the establishment of clear guidelines and policies regarding smartphone use during school hours. Schools can implement policies that restrict the use of smartphones in classrooms or during certain periods of the day, such as instructional time or lunch breaks. By setting these boundaries, schools create an environment that fosters a focused and productive learning environment, reducing the likelihood of excessive smartphone use. These guidelines also serve as a reminder to students that their primary purpose at school is to engage in academic activities, rather than mindlessly scrolling through their devices. In addition, some schools have implemented technological interventions that limit access to certain applications or websites during school hours. This approach, often referred to as app blocking or website filtering, allows schools to control students' access to distracting or inappropriate content. By limiting access to social media platforms, gaming apps, or other time-consuming applications, schools can decrease the instances of excessive smartphone use, improving students' concentration and engagement in academic tasks.

School-based interventions can involve the collaboration of various stakeholders, including teachers, parents, and mental health professionals. For instance, schools may organize workshops or seminars for parents, providing them with strategies to manage their children's smartphone use at home. By involving parents in these interventions, schools create a unified approach aimed at addressing smartphone abuse both at school and at home. This collaborative effort can help reinforce the messages and guidelines established in educational programs or school policies, promoting consistency and coherence in addressing smartphone abuse. Some schools have also incorporated mindfulness or meditation techniques into their intervention strategies. Mindfulness practices promote awareness and self-regulation, allowing students to consciously manage their smartphone use and recognize when it becomes excessive or detrimental to their well-being. Through mindfulness exercises, such as focused breathing or body scans, students can develop a sense of self-control and learn to balance their smartphone usage with other important aspects of their lives, such as social interactions or physical activities. School-based interventions play a crucial role in addressing smartphone abuse among children and adolescents. Educational programs, clear guidelines and policies, technological interventions, collaboration among stakeholders, and mindfulness practices are effective strategies in reducing excessive smartphone use. By implementing these interventions, schools create an environment that promotes healthier relationships with technology and empowers students to make informed choices about their smartphone usage. These interventions are essential in equipping children and adolescents with the necessary skills to navigate the digital world responsibly and maintain their overall well-being.

INCORPORATING DIGITAL LITERACY EDUCATION INTO THE CURRICULUM

This is crucial in equipping students with the necessary skills to navigate the digital world responsibly. From a young age, children and adolescents are exposed to a vast array of digital devices and platforms, making it crucial to provide them with the knowledge and skills to effectively manage and utilize these tools. By incorporating digital literacy education into the curriculum, schools can ensure that students develop competencies in areas such as online safety, critical thinking, and digital citizenship. These skills will not only enable students to make informed decisions about their online presence but also help them understand the potential risks and consequences associated with the digital world. Digital literacy education can also empower students to become creators rather than just consumers of digital content. By teaching them how to create and curate their own digital content, schools can foster creativity and critical thinking skills while also fostering a sense of ownership and responsibility in the digital realm. In addition, incorporating digital literacy education can also promote a more inclusive and equitable learning environment. By teaching students how to use digital tools effectively, schools can bridge the digital divide and ensure that all students have access to the same opportunities and resources. This can help level the playing field and provide students from disadvantaged backgrounds with the skills they need to succeed in an increasingly digital world. Integrating digital literacy education into the curriculum can also enhance overall academic achievement. Research has shown that students who receive digital literacy education perform better academically, as they are more engaged in their learning, have improved problem-solving skills, and are able to access a wide range of resources to support their studies. By equipping students with digital literacy skills, schools can prepare them for the demands of the 21st-century workforce, where digital skills are increasingly in demand. Incorporating digital literacy education into the curriculum is vital in preparing students for the challenges and opportunities of the digital world. By providing them with the necessary skills and knowledge, schools can empower students to navigate the digital landscape responsibly, make informed decisions about their online presence, and become creators rather than just consumers of digital content. By integrating digital literacy education into the curriculum, schools can promote inclusivity, bridge the digital divide, and enhance overall academic achievement. As the digital world continues to evolve and shape our lives, it is imperative that education keeps pace with these changes and equips students with the skills they need to thrive in an increasingly digital society.

RAISING AWARENESS THROUGH WORKSHOPS AND PRESENTATIONS

Another effective strategy to combat smartphone abuse in children and adolescents is by raising awareness through workshops and presentations. These educational sessions seek to inform parents, educators, and the community about the potential dangers of excessive smartphone usage and provide them with the necessary tools to mitigate this issue. Workshops can be designed to cover a wide range of topics, such as the impact of screen time on mental health, the importance of setting healthy boundaries, and the development of digital literacy skills. By actively engaging participants in reflective exercises and interactive discussions, workshops not only enhance knowledge but also encourage critical thinking and problem-solving.

One key objective of these workshops is to educate parents and caregivers about the detrimental effects of excessive smartphone use on their children's overall well-being. Parents are often unaware of the potential risks associated with unlimited access to smartphones, such as cyberbullying, online harassment, and exposure to inappropriate content. Through workshops, they can acquire the understanding and skills needed to protect their children in the digital age. For instance, parents can learn to establish clear rules and boundaries regarding smartphone usage, ensuring that their children have designated periods of screen-free time for activities such as physical exercise, reading, and spending time with family and friends. Workshops can provide guidance on selecting suitable content and age-appropriate apps, so that children can engage with informative and stimulating content while avoiding harmful material. Apart from parents, workshops can also target educators and school staff, as they too play a crucial role in mitigating smartphone abuse among children and adolescents. Teachers can be equipped with the knowledge and techniques necessary to incorporate digital citizenship into their classrooms, promoting responsible and ethical smartphone use. These workshops can emphasize the importance of educating students about online privacy, cyberbullying prevention, and critical evaluation of online information. Workshops can provide educators with resources and strategies to integrate smartphones into the learning process effectively. By embracing the benefits of digital tools while offering guidance on their responsible usage, educators can empower students to become responsible digital citizens.

Another way in which awareness can be raised is through presentations that target the wider community. These presentations can be organized in collaboration with local community centers, schools, and other relevant stakeholders. By educating the community about the risks associated with smartphone abuse, these presentations create a shared responsibility in addressing the issue. Presentations can include real-life stories and case studies to demonstrate the impact of excessive smartphone use on mental health, academic performance, and social interactions. By presenting concrete examples, individuals can better understand the severity of this issue and the importance of taking preventive measures. Presentations can also highlight the benefits of a balanced approach to smartphone use. By showcasing the positive aspects of technology, such as its ability to connect people globally, provide instant access to information, and foster creativity, individuals can appreciate the value that smartphones hold. It is crucial to strike a balance between harnessing the potential of these devices and avoiding their misuse. Presentations can provide practical tips and strategies to help individuals achieve this equilibrium. For instance, individuals can be encouraged to practice digital detoxes periodically, where they voluntarily disconnect from their smartphones for a specified period of time to promote mental well-being and self-reflection.

Raising awareness through workshops and presentations is a valuable strategy to combat smartphone abuse among children and adolescents. These educational initiatives serve to inform and empower parents, educators, and the wider community about the potential dangers of excessive smartphone use. By targeting different stakeholders, workshops can equip parents and caregivers with the necessary tools to protect their children, while also providing educators with strategies to integrate digital citizenship into the classroom. Presentations targeting the community at large create a shared responsibility in addressing the issue and highlight the benefits of a balanced approach to smartphone use. By raising awareness, promoting responsible usage, and fostering critical thinking, society can work towards creating a healthier digital environment for future generations.

COLLABORATING WITH PARENTS AND CAREGIVERS TO REINFORCE BOUNDARIES

Collaborating with parents and caregivers to reinforce boundaries is crucial in addressing smartphone abuse in children and adolescents. Parents play a pivotal role in guiding and supervising their children's smartphone use and can effectively establish and enforce rules and restrictions. It is essential for parents to communicate openly with their children about the potential risks and harms associated with excessive smartphone use. By providing clear explanations, parents can enhance their children's understanding of the need for boundaries and empower them to make responsible choices. In addition, parents should actively monitor their children's smartphone activities, such as by implementing parental control features or regularly checking their device usage. This not only serves as a deterrent for excessive use but also ensures that children are adhering to the established boundaries. Regular conversations with parents about their smartphone use can help children and adolescents reflect on their habits and identify areas for improvement. Parents and caregivers should set a positive example by modeling healthy smartphone behavior themselves. When children see their parents using their smartphones in moderation and prioritizing real-life interactions, they are more likely to emulate such behavior. This collaborative approach between parents and caregivers can effectively reinforce boundaries, promote responsible smartphone use, and ultimately mitigate smartphone abuse among children and adolescents.

CREATING SMARTPHONE-FREE ZONES WITHIN THE SCHOOL PREMISES

Another strategy to combat smartphone abuse in children and adolescents is the creation of smartphone-free zones within the school premises. By designating specific areas where the use of smartphones is not permitted, schools can provide a healthier and more focused environment for learning. These smartphone-free zones could be established in classrooms, libraries, and other common areas where students spend a significant amount of time during the school day. One important benefit of smartphone-free zones is the reduction of distractions. Smartphones are notorious for their ability to divert attention and interrupt concentration. In a school setting, this can be particularly detrimental to the learning experience. By designating certain areas as smartphone-free zones, schools can minimize these distractions and create an environment that is conducive to focused learning. Smartphone-free zones can also foster social interaction among students. The excessive use of smartphones has been linked to a decline in face-to-face communication and interpersonal skills. By creating designated areas where smartphones are not allowed, schools can encourage students to engage in conversation, collaborate on projects, and build meaningful relationships. This can have a positive impact on their social development and overall well-being.

In addition, enforcing smartphone-free zones can help students develop self-regulation skills. Excessive smartphone usage has been linked to impulsivity and a lack of self-control. By setting clear boundaries and rules regarding smartphone use, schools can teach students the importance of self-discipline and self-regulation. This can help them better manage their screen time and develop healthier smartphone habits that will serve them well beyond their school years. Smartphone-free zones can contribute to a safer school environment. The use of smartphones has been linked to an increase in cyberbullying, online harassment, and other negative online interactions. By creating designated areas where smartphones are not permitted, schools can minimize these risks and ensure a safer space for students. This can promote a positive school culture and contribute to the overall well-being of the student body. While some may argue that the creation of smartphone-free zones infringes upon students' rights and personal freedoms, it is important to consider the greater good that such zones can provide. Schools have a duty to create an environment that prioritizes learning, safety, and healthy development. By establishing smartphone-free zones, they are taking a proactive approach to address the issues associated with smartphone abuse. To implement smartphone-free zones effectively, schools should involve students, parents, and staff in the decision-making process. This can ensure that everyone understands the rationale behind the zones and feels a sense of ownership and responsibility. Schools can also provide alternative activities and resources within these zones to further engage students and encourage them to embrace the smartphone-free environment. The creation of smartphone-free zones within the school premises is a valuable strategy to combat smartphone abuse in children and adolescents. By reducing distractions, fostering social interaction, promoting self-regulation skills, contributing to a safer school environment, and prioritizing learning and healthy development, smartphone-free zones offer numerous benefits. It is essential for schools to implement these zones in collaboration with students, parents, and staff to ensure a successful and impactful approach. As smartphone usage continues to rise among young people, it is crucial that schools take proactive steps to address the issue and create a balanced and healthy learning environment for their students.

As technology continues to advance, smartphones have become an integral part of everyday life, especially among children and adolescents. Excessive smartphone use can lead to a range of negative consequences, including impaired cognitive abilities, decreased physical activity, and social isolation. To combat smartphone abuse in this population, several strategies can be employed. Firstly, it is essential to educate parents and guardians about the potential dangers of excessive smartphone use and provide them with guidelines for setting limits on their child's screen time. This may include implementing designated phone-free times, such as during family meals or before bedtime, to encourage interpersonal communication and ensure adequate sleep. Parents can model healthy mobile device usage by limiting their screen time when in the presence of their children. Providing alternative activities that promote physical activity and social interaction, such as sports, hobbies, or community service, can also help divert young individuals' attention away from constant smartphone use. Schools can play a crucial role in combating smartphone addiction by integrating digital literacy programs into their curriculum. These programs would educate students about the responsible use of technology, addressing issues such as appropriate online behavior, digital privacy, and critical evaluation of online information. By fostering critical thinking skills and instilling responsible technology use habits, these programs can empower students to make informed choices regarding smartphone use and mitigate the harmful effects of excessive screen time. Another strategy to combat smartphone abuse is the implementation of smartphone management applications. These applications can be installed on devices, enabling parents and guardians to set predetermined time limits and block certain applications or websites. By utilizing such applications, parents can facilitate responsible smartphone use and prevent their child from falling into the trap of addictive behaviors. Monitoring applications can provide parents with insights into their child's smartphone usage patterns, allowing them to identify any potential problems early on and intervene if necessary. Limiting the availability of smartphones during school hours can also be an effective strategy. Schools can establish policies that restrict smartphone use during instructional time, encouraging students to be fully present and engaged in their educational activities. This would reduce distractions and offer a conducive learning environment while promoting face-to-face interactions among students. Public health campaigns and awareness programs can also play a vital role in combating smartphone addiction in children and adolescents. These campaigns can raise awareness about the potential dangers of excessive smartphone use and provide information on healthy ways to manage screen time. By reaching out to parents, educators, and the broader community, these initiatives can foster a collective effort to mitigate the negative impact of smartphone addiction in young individuals. Addressing the issue of smartphone abuse among children and adolescents requires a multi-faceted approach involving parents, schools, and society as a whole. By implementing strategies such as educating parents, integrating digital literacy programs, uti-lizing smartphone management applications, establishing school policies, and conducting public health campaigns, it is possible to combat smartphone addiction and promote healthier habits among youth. Through these efforts, we can ensure that smartphones remain valuable tools rather than harmful addic-tions in the lives of young individuals.

VI. COMMUNITY AND GOVERNMENTAL INITIATIVES TO TACKLE SMARTPHONE ABUSE

In order to effectively address the growing issue of smartphone abuse among children and adolescents, it is vital for communities and governments to take necessary initiatives. Firstly, community-based organizations can play a crucial role in raising awareness about the negative consequences of excessive smartphone use. This can be done through educational campaigns that target schools, parents, and community members. For instance, local community centers can offer workshops and seminars to educate parents on healthy smartphone use, the importance of setting limits, and the potential risks associated with smartphone addiction. Community organizations can collaborate with schools to implement comprehensive educational programs that promote responsible smartphone use among students. These programs can include classroom lessons, informational materials, and parent engagement activities to ensure a holistic approach towards tackling smartphone abuse. Governmental initiatives are pivotal in addressing smartphone abuse on a broader scale. Legislative measures can be introduced to regulate the marketing and sale of smartphones to children and adolescents. For example, age restrictions can be imposed on the purchase of smartphones, similar to regulations placed on other products such as alcohol and tobacco. This would discourage parents from buying smartphones for their young children, who may not possess the necessary maturity to handle such technology responsibly. Governments can allocate funding for research and prevention programs aimed at understanding the effects of smartphone abuse on children and adolescents. This would enable scientists and researchers to conduct extensive studies on this issue, further generating awareness and providing evidence-based recommendations for addressing the problem. Governments can work closely with healthcare professionals to develop guidelines and protocols for screening and treating smartphone addiction in children and adolescents. Primary care physicians and mental health practitioners can be trained to identify symptoms of smartphone abuse and provide appropriate intervention strategies. Such initiatives can also involve establishing specialized clinics or centers where young individuals struggling with smartphone addiction can receive professional help. Telehealth services can be integrated to make treatment more accessible to those in remote areas or who are unable to seek in-person consultations. Governments can collaborate with healthcare professionals and technology companies to develop smartphone applications or tools that encourage responsible smartphone use and provide support to individuals who are trying to cut back on their usage.

In addition to community and governmental initiatives, schools can also play a significant role in addressing smartphone abuse among students. Schools can implement policies that restrict smartphone use during instructional hours, thereby creating a focused learning environment free from distractions. Strict enforcement of these policies, coupled with clear communication to parents and students, would reinforce the importance of responsible smartphone use. Schools can incorporate digital literacy programs into their curriculum, teaching students about the potential risks and benefits of smartphone use, as well as strategies for maintaining a healthy balance. By integrating such programs, schools can equip students with the skills to make informed decisions regarding their smartphone usage, ensuring they develop responsible habits from an early age. Addressing the issue of smartphone abuse among children and adolescents requires a multi-faceted approach involving community, governmental, and educational initiatives. Community organizations can raise awareness and provide education to parents and community members, while schools can implement policies and programs to promote responsible smartphone use. Governments can take legislative measures, allocate funding for research and prevention programs, and collaborate with healthcare professionals to develop guidelines and treatment protocols. By working together, these initiatives can combat smartphone abuse and empower young individuals to use their smartphones responsibly, fostering a healthier and more balanced relationship with technology.

RAISING PUBLIC AWARENESS THROUGH CAMPAIGNS AND ADVERTISEMENTS

One effective strategy to combat smartphone abuse in children and adolescents is by raising public awareness through campaigns and advertisements. By increasing awareness of the potential dangers and negative impacts of excessive smartphone use, society can better equip parents, educators, and policymakers to address this issue. Campaigns and advertisements can serve as powerful tools to disseminate information, convey key messages, and promote behavior change. For instance, public service announcements aired on television, radio, and social media platforms can effectively reach a wide audience and educate them about the detrimental effects of smartphone addiction. These campaigns can focus on highlighting the various consequences of excessive smartphone use, such as decreased academic performance, impaired social skills, and mental health issues like anxiety and depression. A compelling advertisement could showcase the detrimental effects of smartphone addiction on personal relationships, portraying a scenario where a child constantly ignores their friends and family to scroll through their device. The emotional impact of such advertisements can grab the viewers' attention, making them more receptive to the message being conveyed. Campaigns and advertisements can provide practical tips and strategies for parents and caregivers to limit smartphone use among children. These can include setting time limits for screen usage, encouraging outdoor activities, and promoting face-to-face interactions rather than relying solely on digital communication. By emphasizing the importance of balance and moderation, these campaigns can help parents and caregivers establish healthy boundaries surrounding smartphone use. Campaigns and advertisements can call for stricter regulations on marketing strategies employed by smartphone manufacturers. The majority of smartphone apps and games are designed to be highly addictive, employing psychological tactics such as push notifications and constantly refreshed feeds to keep users engaged. By drawing attention to these manipulative techniques, campaigns can advocate for measures that protect vulnerable children and adolescents from falling into the trap of excessive smartphone use. These measures can include age restrictions on certain apps, mandatory warnings on addictive content, and parental controls built into devices. Campaigns and advertisements can enlist celebrity endorsements and testimonials from individuals who have successfully overcome smartphone addiction. These personal stories can serve as powerful motivators and inspire individuals to take action and make positive changes in their own lives. In addition to traditional campaigns, social media platforms can also play a pivotal role in raising public awareness about smartphone abuse. Influencers and organizations can leverage their online presence to share educational content, personal experiences, and practical strategies for tackling smartphone addiction. Hashtags and challenges can be used to engage and motivate individuals to actively participate in reducing smartphone abuse. Collaborations with schools and educational institutions can be instrumental in educating students about responsible smartphone use. Guest speakers, workshops, and structured programs can provide students with the tools and knowledge necessary to navigate the digital world in a healthy and balanced manner. Raising public awareness through campaigns and advertisements can be a potent method to combat smartphone abuse in children and adolescents. By informing and educating individuals about the negative consequences of excessive smartphone use, these initiatives can empower parents, educators, and policymakers to take proactive measures in their respective domains. By advocating for stricter regulations on marketing strategies employed by smartphone manufacturers, campaigns can protect vulnerable individuals from falling prey to addictive apps and games. By utilizing social media platforms and collaborating with educational institutions, these awareness initiatives can effectively reach the target audience and promote behavior change. Through these collective efforts, society can strive towards a future where children and teenagers can harness the benefits of smartphones while maintaining a healthy and balanced relationship with technology.

PROVIDING EDUCATIONAL RESOURCES TO PARENTS AND ADOLESCENTS

This is a crucial step in combating smartphone abuse among children and adolescents. It is important for parents to understand the potential dangers of excessive smartphone use and to be equipped with strategies to manage their child's smartphone habits effectively. One useful resource that can be provided to parents is information on the negative effects of excessive screen time on cognitive development, mental health, and social skills. This information can be disseminated through seminars, workshops, or online platforms and should highlight the importance of setting limits and boundaries for smartphone use. Educational resources should emphasize the significance of parental involvement in monitoring and regulating smartphone use. Parents should be encouraged to have open and honest conversations with their children about the risks associated with excessive screen time and to establish clear rules regarding when and how smartphones can be used. By providing parents with the necessary knowledge and tools to manage their child's smartphone use, we can empower them to take an active role in promoting healthy habits and behaviors. It is equally important to provide educational resources directly to adolescents to increase their awareness and understanding of the potential harms of smartphone overuse. Such resources could include informative videos, interactive workshops, or educational apps that are specifically designed to educate teenagers about the dangers of smartphone addiction. These resources should address the negative impact of excessive screen time on mental health, sleep patterns, academic performance, and social interactions. They should also promote alternative activities and hobbies that can help adolescents develop a healthy balance between screen time and other aspects of life. In addition to providing educational resources, it is essential to teach parents and adolescents about the importance of digital literacy. This includes educating them about online privacy, cyberbullying, and the potential dangers associated with sharing personal information on social media platforms. Digital literacy training can help parents and adolescents develop the necessary skills to navigate the online world safely and responsibly. It can also empower them to make informed decisions about the apps, websites, and content they engage with on their smartphones. Collaborating with schools and community organizations can be an effective way to implement educational resources on smartphone abuse prevention. Schools can play a key role in raising awareness by integrating this topic into the curriculum and organizing informative sessions for both parents and students. Partnering with community organizations such as youth centers or counseling services can provide access to expert guidance and support. These organizations can organize workshops or group sessions where parents and adolescents can learn from professionals and share their experiences with peers facing similar challenges. Monitoring and evaluating the effectiveness of these educational resources is crucial to ensure their impact on reducing smartphone abuse. Surveys, interviews, and focus groups can be conducted to gather feedback from parents and adolescents on the usefulness and effectiveness of the provided resources. This feedback can be used to identify areas of improvement and to tailor future educational initiatives based on the specific needs of the target audience.

Providing educational resources to parents and adolescents is a necessary step in combating smartphone abuse among children and adolescents. These resources should focus on raising awareness about the negative effects of excessive screen time, promoting parental involvement, teaching digital literacy skills, and offering alternative activities. Collaboration with schools and community organizations will facilitate the implementation of these resources, while monitoring and evaluating their effectiveness will ensure continuous improvement. By equipping parents and adolescents with the necessary knowledge and tools, we can empower them to mitigate the risks associated with smartphone abuse and promote healthy smartphone habits.

REGULATING SMARTPHONE ADVERTISING TARGETING CHILDREN AND ADOLESCENTS

Regulating smartphone advertising targeting children and adolescents is another crucial strategy in combating smartphone abuse. Smartphone advertising plays a significant role in influencing the behavior and choices of children and adolescents. Advertisements specifically targeted towards this vulnerable age group often use persuasive techniques to manipulate their preferences and create a constant desire for the latest gadgets and apps. These advertisements exploit their innate curiosity and desire for social acceptance, leading to excessive smartphone use. Implementing regulations on smartphone advertising aimed at children and adolescents is necessary to protect their well-being and ensure responsible marketing practices.

To start with, government agencies must collaborate with advertising companies to establish strict guidelines and ethical standards for advertisements targeting young audiences. These guidelines should emphasize the need to promote healthy smartphone use and discourage excessive screen time. Advertisements should not exploit the ignorance and vulnerability of children and adolescents by making false or exaggerated claims about the benefits of their products. The use of manipulative tactics, such as creating a sense of urgency or tapping into social insecurities, should be strictly prohibited. By implementing these guidelines, it will be possible to ensure that advertisements aimed at children and adolescents are transparent, honest, and promote responsible smartphone use. Given the influence of social media platforms on young audiences, these regulations must extend to advertisements displayed within apps and social media sites. It is crucial to address the pervasive nature of targeted advertisements on platforms such as Facebook and Instagram. These platforms collect data on users' preferences and behaviors and use this information to deliver personalized ads. Consequently, children and adolescents are constantly exposed to advertisements that align with their interests and desires, thereby intensifying their smartphone addiction. By regulating these targeted advertisements to ensure they align with ethical marketing practices, their impact on shaping young minds can be significantly reduced. In addition to regulations, educational campaigns targeting both children and parents should be implemented to increase awareness and develop critical thinking skills regarding smartphone advertisements. Children and adolescents need to be educated about the intention behind advertising and how it can influence their behavior. By teaching them to question the claims made in advertisements and deciphering their underlying messages, they can become more resistant to manipulative tactics used by advertisers. Parents also play a crucial role in this process and should be provided with resources and guidance on discussing advertising with their children. Empowering parents with knowledge and tools to navigate the world of smartphone advertising can alleviate the pressure on children and adolescents to constantly seek the latest devices and apps.

It is essential to establish a robust system of monitoring and enforcing these regulations. Government regulatory bodies should conduct regular audits and evaluations of advertisements, ensuring compliance with the established guidelines. Strict penalties should be imposed on advertisers found to be in violation of these regulations, including heavy fines and the temporary suspension of advertising privileges. By creating an environment where responsible marketing practices are enforced, advertisers will be more cautious in their approaches, thus reducing the negative impact of smartphone advertising on children and adolescents.

While regulating smartphone advertising targeting children and adolescents is an essential strategy, it is crucial to strike a balance that allows for innovation and growth in the industry. The aim should not be to eliminate advertisements entirely but to ensure they are ethical, transparent, and conducive to healthy smartphone use in young individuals. Advertisements can still provide valuable information and promote products or services that enhance children's learning and development. The regulatory framework should identify and support advertising that aligns with positive child and adolescent outcomes, fostering a symbiotic relationship between responsible marketing practices and the well-being of young smartphone users.

Regulating smartphone advertising targeted towards children and adolescents is a vital strategy in combating smartphone abuse. By implementing strict guidelines, leveraging educational campaigns, and establishing robust monitoring and enforcement systems, the negative impact of advertisements on young minds can be significantly reduced. It is important to strike a balance between regulation and innovation, allowing for responsible marketing practices that contribute to the positive development of children and adolescents. Through these measures, the prevalence of smartphone addiction in young individuals can be curbed, ensuring their well-being and promoting healthy smartphone use.

PROMOTING ALTERNATIVE RECREATIONAL ACTIVITIES THROUGH COMMUNITY PROGRAMS

Community programs play a crucial role in promoting alternative recreational activities for children and adolescents. As previously mentioned, physical inactivity and sedentary behavior have become major concerns in today's society, and community programs can help combat this issue by offering a variety of engaging activities. One effective strategy is to provide opportunities for children and adolescents to participate in organized sports. Not only do sports provide a fun and exciting way to stay active, but they also promote important values such as teamwork, discipline, and perseverance. By joining sports teams or leagues, young individuals can develop a sense of belonging and camaraderie, which can contribute to their overall well-being. Community programs can also organize outdoor activities that encourage children and adolescents to connect with nature. For instance, hiking, camping, and biking are excellent options that allow young individuals to appreciate the beauty of the natural world while engaging in physical exercise. Community programs can promote the arts as a recreational activity. Activities such as painting, dancing, or playing a musical instrument not only help children and adolescents express their creativity but also provide opportunities for self-expression and personal growth. Engaging in artistic activities has been shown to have a positive impact on mental health, reducing symptoms of anxiety and depression. Community programs can also offer classes or workshops on topics such as cooking, photography, or gardening, which can spark young individuals' interest in new hobbies and provide them with valuable life skills. These alternative recreational activities not only provide a healthy alternative to screen time but also contribute to the social and emotional well-being of children and adolescents, fostering personal growth and development. Community programs play a vital role in promoting a balanced and active lifestyle among the younger population.

In today's modern society, screens have become an integral part of our lives, with smartphones being one of the most prevalent devices in the hands of both children and adolescents. This newfound reliance on smartphones has raised concerns about the potential negative effects of excessive screen time on the development and well-being of young individuals. As stated earlier in this essay, excessive smartphone use can lead to addictive behaviors, social isolation, and poor mental health outcomes. It is therefore crucial for parents, educators, and policymakers to implement strategies that combat smartphone abuse in children and adolescents. One effective strategy to combat smartphone abuse is to educate parents about the potential risks and realities of excessive screen time. Many parents may be unaware of the negative consequences associated with their children's prolonged smartphone use. By providing them with comprehensive information about the impact of excessive screen time on cognitive, social, and emotional development, parents will be better equipped to set appropriate limits and boundaries for their children's smartphone use. Educating parents should also involve emphasizing the importance of modeling healthy screen behaviour at home. Children often mirror the habits and behaviours of their parents, and if parents are constantly glued to their smartphones, children are likely to do the same. By promoting a balanced approach to screen usage within the family, parents can instill healthy habits in their children from an early age.

Another key strategy is to incorporate digital literacy programs into school curricula. As smartphones become increasingly integrated into educational settings, it is essential to equip students with the necessary skills to navigate the digital world responsibly. These programs should focus on teaching students about online safety, privacy, and the potential consequences of their actions in the digital realm. When students are educated about the potential risks associated with excessive smartphone use, they are more likely to make informed choices and exercise self-regulation. In addition to promoting responsible smartphone use, these programs should also emphasize the importance of offline activities such as physical exercise, face-to-face communication, and creative outlets. By providing students with a well-rounded education that includes digital literacy, schools can play a pivotal role in cultivating healthy behaviours and attitudes towards smartphone use. Policymakers should consider implementing regulations and guidelines to protect young individuals from the negative effects of excessive screen time. For example, some countries have introduced measures that limit the sale of smartphones to children under a certain age or restrict access to specific apps and websites known for their addictive qualities. While it is essential to strike a balance between protecting young individuals and promoting freedom of choice, these regulations can serve as a starting point for parents and children to have open discussions about responsible smartphone use. By setting clear limits and expectations, policymakers can help shape a society that values the benefits of technology while recognizing the need for healthy boundaries. It is crucial to foster open communication and collaboration between parents, educators, and children themselves. By creating a supportive and non-judgmental environment, children and adolescents will feel more comfortable discussing their smartphone habits, concerns, and challenges. This open dialogue can help parents and educators understand the underlying reasons for excessive smartphone use and identify potential triggers or stressors. By working together, parents and educators can develop personalized strategies tailored to each child's needs. These strategies can include setting specific screen-free times, encouraging alternative activities, and creating a technology-free bedroom environment. By involving children and adolescents in the decision-making process, they will feel a sense of ownership over their smartphone use and be more invested in adhering to the established guidelines.

Combating smartphone abuse in children and adolescents requires a multi-faceted approach involving parents, educators, policymakers, and young individuals themselves. By educating parents about the risks of excessive screen time, incorporating digital literacy programs into schools, implementing regulations and guidelines, and fostering open communication, society can work together to create a healthier relationship with smartphones. Only by addressing this issue collectively can we ensure that the benefits of technology are maximized while minimizing the potential negative consequences on the well-being and development of young individuals.

VII. THE ROLE OF MENTAL HEALTH PROFESSIONALS IN ADDRESSING SMARTPHONE ABUSE

In addition to the efforts of parents and schools, mental health professionals play a crucial role in addressing smartphone abuse among children and adolescents. These professionals possess the knowledge and expertise to assess and diagnose individuals struggling with addiction and mental health issues related to smartphone use. They can provide individual therapy to help young people understand the underlying reasons for their excessive smartphone use and develop healthier coping mechanisms. Group therapy sessions allow adolescents to connect with peers facing similar challenges, fostering a sense of support and understanding. Mental health professionals can guide parents in establishing appropriate boundaries and rules regarding smartphone usage, offering strategies to monitor and limit screen time effectively. They can educate parents about the potential dangers and consequences of smartphone abuse, such as cyberbullying, online predators, and negative impacts on academic performance and social relationships. By addressing smartphone abuse comprehensively, mental health professionals ensure that young individuals receive the support and tools necessary to regain control over their smartphone use and restore balance in their lives.

ASSESSING AND DIAGNOSING SMARTPHONE ADDICTION IN CHILDREN AND ADOLESCENTS

Assessing and diagnosing smartphone addiction in children and adolescents is crucial for developing appropriate interventions and strategies. There are multiple assessment tools and techniques that can be utilized to determine the severity of smartphone addiction in this population. One commonly used tool is the Smartphone Addiction Scale (SAS), which measures various dimensions of smartphone use such as withdrawal, compulsive behaviors, and functional impairment. The SAS has been found to have high reliability and validity in both clinical and research settings, making it a valuable instrument for assessing smartphone addiction in children and adolescents. Diagnostic interviews can be conducted to gather in-depth information about the individual's smartphone use patterns and associated problems. These interviews can be structured or semi-structured and provide clinicians with valuable insights into the psychological and social consequences of excessive smartphone use. Collaborative assessment approaches involving parents, teachers, and other significant individuals in the child or adolescent's life can also be employed to obtain a comprehensive understanding of the individual's smartphone addiction. This multi-source assessment not only enhances the accuracy of the diagnosis but also allows for a more holistic treatment approach. It is important to consider the developmental context in which smartphone addiction occurs to ensure accurate assessment and diagnosis. For instance, the DSM-5, a widely used diagnostic manual, acknowledges that symptoms of addiction may manifest differently in children and adolescents compared to adults. Specific criteria and assessment measures that account for age-related differences should be used when evaluating smartphone addiction in this population. Cultural factors should also be taken into account, as norms surrounding smartphone use may vary across different cultural contexts. In some cultures, excessive smartphone use may be more socially acceptable and may not be viewed as problematic, making it important to consider cultural norms and values when assessing and diagnosing smartphone addiction in children and adolescents. Assessing and diagnosing smartphone addiction in children and adolescents requires the use of valid and reliable assessment tools, diagnostic interviews, collaborative approaches, and consideration of developmental and cultural factors. By accurately diagnosing smartphone addiction, healthcare professionals can intervene at an early stage to prevent further escalation of the problem and design effective treatment strategies. It is essential to recognize that smartphone addiction is a complex and multifaceted issue, requiring a comprehensive understanding of the individual's unique circumstances and context. Ongoing research and collaboration between researchers, clinicians, and educators are crucial to furthering our understanding of smartphone addiction in children and adolescents and developing effective interventions to combat this growing problem.

PROVIDING INDIVIDUAL AND FAMILY THERAPY FOR AFFECTED INDIVIDUALS

In addition to implementing preventive measures and addressing the environmental factors contributing to smartphone abuse, it is crucial to provide individual and family therapy for affected individuals. Individual therapy can be an effective method to help children and adolescents develop healthier habits and cope with the negative effects of excessive smartphone use. This form of therapy allows for a one-on-one setting with a trained therapist who can provide personalized treatment plans based on the specific needs of each individual. Through individual therapy, therapists can work with the affected individuals to identify the underlying issues leading to smartphone abuse, such as anxiety, depression, or low self-esteem. By addressing these root causes, therapists can help individuals shift their focus away from their smartphones and develop healthier coping mechanisms.

Family therapy is another essential component in combating smartphone abuse in children and adolescents. Given that smartphone abuse often affects the entire family by disrupting communication and fostering disconnection, involving the family in the treatment process is crucial. Family therapy can help improve communication and strengthen family bonds, creating a supportive and understanding environment where open dialogue can take place. During family therapy sessions, therapists can educate parents and siblings about the potential dangers and consequences of excessive smartphone use. By fostering empathy and understanding, family therapy can help family members work together to set limits on smartphone use and establish healthy digital boundaries. Family therapy can help parents develop effective parenting strategies and tools to monitor and regulate their children's smartphone use.

One approach that has shown promise in family therapy is the use of the Systemic Family Therapy (SFT) model. SFT is an evidence-based therapeutic approach that focuses on understanding the dynamics and patterns within a family system. This approach aims to identify the roles and interactions of each family member and how these contribute to the problem at hand. By helping families recognize and challenge dysfunctional patterns, SFT can guide them towards healthier ways of relating and coping with smartphone abuse. For example, therapists using SFT may encourage families to engage in joint activities that promote face-to-face interaction, such as family outings or game nights, to counterbalance excessive screen time.

In addition to individual and family therapy, group therapy can be an effective tool to provide support and help individuals realize that they are not alone in their struggles with smartphone abuse. Group therapy offers a unique platform where individuals can share their experiences, offer support, and learn from one another's coping strategies. By participating in group therapy sessions, individuals can gain insight into how their smartphone use has affected their lives and develop new skills to overcome their addiction. Through the camaraderie and empathetic environment of the group, individuals can find the encouragement and motivation they need to reduce their smartphone use and establish healthier habits. Incorporating therapeutic techniques such as Cognitive-Behavioral Therapy (CBT) can enhance the efficacy of individual and family therapy interventions for smartphone abuse. CBT focuses on helping individuals identify and challenge negative thoughts and behaviors. Therapists can work with affected individuals to reframe their beliefs and attitudes towards smartphone use, allowing them to gain control over their habits. By teaching individuals healthy coping mechanisms and stress management techniques, CBT can aid in reducing the reliance on smartphones as a means of escape or self-soothing. Providing individual and family therapy is crucial to effectively combat smartphone abuse in children and adolescents. Individual therapy allows for personalized treatment plans to address the underlying issues contributing to excessive smartphone use. On the other hand, family therapy creates a supportive environment where families can work together to set limits on smartphone use and establish healthy digital boundaries. Group therapy and incorporating therapeutic techniques like Cognitive-Behavioral Therapy enhance the effectiveness of these interventions. By implementing these strategies, individuals can gain the necessary skills and support to overcome smartphone addiction and lead balanced and fulfilling lives.

OFFERING PSYCHOEDUCATION ON HEALTHY SMARTPHONE USE HABITS

In addition to the aforementioned strategies, offering psychoeducation on healthy smartphone use habits can be an effective method to combat smartphone abuse in children and adolescents. Psychoeducation refers to the provision of information and educational resources regarding mental health and well-being, with the goal of empowering individuals to make informed decisions and adopt healthier behaviors. In the context of smartphone use, psychoeducation can play a crucial role in helping children and adolescents understand the potential risks and benefits associated with their device usage, as well as providing them with strategies to develop healthier habits.

One key component of psychoeducation on healthy smartphone use habits is helping children and adolescents become aware of the negative consequences of excessive smartphone use. Many young individuals may not fully understand the impact that excessive screen time can have on their physical and mental health. By providing them with accurate information about the potential risks, such as sleep disturbances, decreased physical activity, and negative effects on mental well-being, they can become more motivated to adopt healthier habits. For example, they may be more inclined to limit their screen time in order to prioritize activities like exercise, face-to-face interactions, and sleep.

Psychoeducation can help children and adolescents identify their specific risk factors for smartphone abuse. This can include factors such as boredom, loneliness, low self-esteem, or difficulties in regulating emotions. By understanding these underlying factors, young individuals can gain insight into the reasons behind their excessive smartphone use and develop healthier coping mechanisms. For instance, those who use their smartphones to cope with boredom can be encouraged to explore alternative activities such as reading, playing a musical instrument, or engaging in a hobby that aligns with their interests. By addressing the root causes of smartphone abuse, psychoeducation can help children and adolescents build healthier habits and reduce their reliance on their devices. Psychoeducation can provide children and adolescents with practical strategies to develop healthy smartphone usage habits. This can include setting boundaries and establishing clear rules around screen time, such as limiting the use of devices during mealtimes or before bedtime. By providing concrete guidelines, young individuals can have a clearer understanding of what constitutes appropriate smartphone use. Psychoeducation can educate them on the importance of taking regular breaks from their devices, as well as engaging in other activities that promote well-being, such as spending time outdoors, pursuing hobbies, or engaging in physical exercise. Psychoeducation can also address the issue of cyberbullying and promote safe online behaviors. Children and adolescents may be unaware of the potential dangers associated with sharing personal information online or engaging in harmful behaviors towards others. Through psychoeducation, young individuals can gain a better understanding of the consequences of cyberbullying and the importance of treating others with respect and empathy in online interactions. By promoting safe online behaviors, psychoeducation can help mitigate the negative effects of smartphone use and create a healthier digital environment for children and adolescents. Offering psychoeducation on healthy smartphone use habits can be a valuable strategy to combat smartphone abuse in children and adolescents. By providing them with accurate information about the risks associated with excessive smartphone use, helping them identify underlying risk factors, and equipping them with practical strategies to develop healthier habits, psychoeducation can empower young individuals to make informed decisions and take control of their smartphone usage. By integrating psychoeducation into school curriculums and engaging parents and caregivers in the process, the potential for long-term positive change in smartphone use habits can be maximized. By promoting healthier smartphone use, young individuals can cultivate a more balanced relationship with their devices and enhance their overall well-being.

COLLABORATING WITH OTHER PROFESSIONALS TO DEVELOP COMPREHENSIVE TREATMENT PLANS

Collaboration among professionals is crucial when developing comprehensive treatment plans to combat smartphone abuse in children and adolescents. This collaboration involves various professionals including psychologists, counselors, educators, and parents. Each professional brings unique expertise and perspectives to the table, contributing to a holistic treatment approach. Psychologists play a vital role in understanding the underlying psychological factors that contribute to smartphone addiction. Through assessments and therapy, they can identify any underlying mental health issues such as anxiety or depression that may be exacerbating smartphone abuse. By collaborating with counselors, these professionals can create tailored treatment plans that address both the psychological and addictive aspects of smartphone use. Counselors, on the other hand, provide essential guidance and support to individuals and families struggling with smartphone addiction. Their expertise in addiction counseling helps individuals develop healthier coping mechanisms and establish boundaries when it comes to smartphone usage. By collaborating with psychologists, counselors can gain deeper insight into the psychological underpinnings of smartphone addiction, allowing for a more comprehensive treatment approach. Educators play a crucial role in interventions and prevention efforts targeted at addressing smartphone abuse in educational settings.

Through collaboration with psychologists and counselors, educators can design age-appropriate curricula that increase students' awareness of the potential dangers associated with excessive smartphone use. This collaborative approach ensures that educators are equipped with the necessary tools and strategies to support students in developing healthy relationships with technology. Parents' involvement and collaboration with professionals are paramount in the treatment process. Open communication between parents and professionals fosters a supportive environment that encourages accountability, understanding, and progress. By actively engaging in collaborative discussions, parents gain valuable insights into the factors that contribute to smartphone abuse and learn effective strategies to set boundaries and manage their child's smartphone usage. They can also help reinforce therapeutic interventions at home, creating a consistent and supportive environment. Collaboration among professionals is essential to developing comprehensive treatment plans for addressing smartphone abuse in children and adolescents. The collective knowledge, skills, and expertise of psychologists, counselors, educators, and parents ensure that treatment plans are tailored to the individual's needs, encompassing both the psychological and addictive aspects of smartphone use. Through collaboration, professionals can develop a cohesive approach, allowing for a more effective and holistic treatment process. By involving various stakeholders, the chances of long-term success in combating smartphone abuse are significantly increased, leading to healthier technology habits and improved overall well-being in children and adolescents.

As screens have become increasingly prevalent in today's society, concerns about smartphone abuse in children and adolescents have grown. This essay aims to explore strategies to combat this issue and provide insights into the potential consequences of excessive screen time. Firstly, it is crucial to recognize the negative impacts of smartphone abuse on children and adolescents. Research has shown that excessive screen time can lead to various physical and mental health problems, such as obesity, sleep disturbances, and symptoms of anxiety and depression. Prolonged exposure to screens can negatively affect cognitive development, attention span, and academic performance. With these concerns in mind, it becomes essential to implement strategies that promote healthy screen habits. One strategy is to establish clear boundaries and guidelines for screen use. Parents and guardians should set daily time limits and establish specific periods during which screen use is not allowed, such as mealtimes or before bedtime. By establishing these boundaries, children and adolescents can learn to balance their screen time with other activities, such as physical exercise, socializing, or engaging in hobbies.

Parents should lead by example and adhere to the same guidelines they set for their children. If adults display responsible screen habits, children are more likely to follow suit.

In addition to setting boundaries, it is crucial to encourage alternative activities that promote physical and mental well-being. Children and adolescents should be provided with opportunities for physical exercise, such as playing sports or engaging in outdoor activities. Encouraging participation in hobbies or creative pursuits, such as painting, playing an instrument, or writing, can help divert attention away from screens and foster personal growth. Fostering social interactions through family activities, outings with friends, or participation in community events can reduce the reliance on smartphones as a means of social connection. Another effective strategy to combat smartphone abuse is to create technology-free zones. Designating specific areas in the house where screens are not allowed can help reduce the amount of time spent on smartphones. For instance, the dining table and bedrooms can be designated as technology-free zones, allowing for more meaningful family interactions and promoting healthy sleep habits. Schools and communities can implement policies that limit smartphone use during certain periods or in specific areas, such as classrooms or libraries.

Education plays a vital role in combating smartphone abuse. Children and adolescents should be educated about the potential consequences of excessive screen time. Educators and parents should emphasize the importance of responsible digital citizenship, teaching young people about online safety, appropriate online behavior, and the potential dangers of excessive screen time. Teaching children about the benefits of face-to-face communication, critical thinking, and problem-solving skills can help them develop a more balanced approach to screen use.

Parental involvement and communication are crucial in addressing smartphone abuse. Parents should engage in open and honest conversations with their children about the potential risks and benefits of smartphones. By maintaining a supportive and non-judgmental approach, parents can create an environment where their children feel comfortable discussing their screen habits. Parents should monitor their children's screen activities, using parental control apps or software to limit access to inappropriate content. Regular check-ins and discussions about screen time can facilitate ongoing dialogue and encourage responsible screen habits. It is vital to provide support and resources to individuals struggling with smartphone addiction. Mental health professionals, educators, and parents should work together to identify signs of smartphone addiction and provide appropriate interventions. Implementing school-based programs that educate students on the dangers of smartphone abuse and provide coping strategies can be beneficial. Providing access to support groups or therapy can offer individuals struggling with smartphone addiction a safe space to share their experiences and receive necessary guidance. Combating smartphone abuse in children and adolescents requires a multifaceted approach that encompasses setting boundaries, promoting alternative activities, creating technology-free zones, educating individuals, fostering parental involvement, and providing support and resources. By implementing these strategies, we can help children and adolescents develop healthy screen habits, mitigate potential negative consequences, and promote overall well-being. It is crucial for society as a whole to recognize the importance of this issue and work together to address it effectively.

VIII. DIRECTIONS IN COMBATING SMARTPHONE ABUSE IN CHILDREN AND ADOLESCENTS

Despite the advancements made in understanding and addressing smartphone abuse in children and adolescents, several research gaps still exist, necessitating further investigation and exploration. One key area that requires attention is the long-term effects of smartphone abuse on the psychological well-being of young individuals. While previous studies have examined the immediate effects of excessive smartphone use, such as increased anxiety and decreased sleep quality, the long-term consequences remain largely understudied. Future research should focus on determining the lasting impact of smartphone abuse on mental health outcomes, such as depression, self-esteem, and social anxiety, to better grasp the potential implications for children's and adolescents' overall well-being.

Another research gap pertains to the efficacy of interventions aimed at reducing smartphone abuse. Although various strategies have been proposed and implemented, there is limited evidence regarding their effectiveness and long-term sustainability. Future studies should rigorously evaluate the outcomes of different intervention approaches, including educational programs, parental guidance, and cognitive-behavioral therapy, to determine their impact on reducing smartphone abuse and promoting healthier smartphone habits in children and adolescents. This research should also consider the specific factors that enhance or hinder the success of such interventions, such as age, gender, socioeconomic status, and cultural background, to tailor interventions accordingly and ensure optimal results.

Advancing our understanding of the underlying mechanisms and motivations driving smartphone abuse in young individuals is crucial. Identifying the factors that contribute to excessive smartphone use, such as social media engagement, gaming, or instant messaging, can inform the development of targeted interventions. Exploring the role of personality traits, such as impulsivity and self-control, in smartphone abuse can provide valuable insights into potential risk factors and help identify individuals who may be more vulnerable to developing problematic behaviors. Examining the impact of peer influence and societal pressures on smartphone use can further enhance our understanding of the complex dynamics involved in this phenomenon.

Another key research gap relates to the influence of parental modeling and family dynamics on children's and adolescents' smartphone use. While studies have indicated that parental smartphone use patterns significantly impact their children's behavior, further research is needed to explore the underlying processes and mechanisms involved. Particularly, investigating the role of parental monitoring, communication, and the establishment of rules and boundaries can shed light on effective strategies for parents to manage and prevent smartphone abuse in their children. Understanding the impact of family dynamics, such as parenting styles, sibling relationships, and family cohesion, can also contribute to the development of comprehensive prevention and intervention programs.

As technology continues to evolve rapidly, it is crucial to

continually update research models and methodologies to keep pace with these advancements. Traditional research methodologies, such as self-report questionnaires and observational studies, have limitations in capturing the intricate and dynamic nature of smartphone use. Embracing novel approaches, such as ecological momentary assessment and objective measures of smartphone engagement, can provide a more accurate and comprehensive understanding of smartphone abuse in real-world contexts. Employing longitudinal designs can help trace the developmental trajectories of smartphone abuse and identify critical periods for intervention and prevention.

While significant progress has been made in combating smartphone abuse in children and adolescents, several research gaps persist, necessitating further investigation and exploration. Understanding the long-term effects of smartphone abuse, evaluating the efficacy of interventions, uncovering the underlying mechanisms, examining parental influence, and utilizing innovative research methodologies are crucial directions for future research. By addressing these gaps, we can advance our knowledge, inform prevention and intervention strategies, and ultimately protect the well-being of young individuals in the digital age.

LONGITUDINAL STUDIES TO ASSESS THE LONG-TERM EFFECTS OF SMARTPHONE ADDICTION

A significant contribution to understanding the long-term effects of smartphone addiction can be made through longitudinal studies. These studies involve observing a group of individuals over an extended period to identify patterns, trends, and changes in their behavior and health. By employing this research approach, researchers can overcome some of the limitations associated with cross-sectional studies, which only provide a snapshot of data at a specific point in time. Longitudinal studies can provide a more comprehensive understanding of the long-term consequences of smartphone addiction by examining how it evolves and manifests over time. One of the primary advantages of conducting longitudinal studies is the ability to track the progression and stability of smartphone addiction. By following a cohort of individuals from early childhood or adolescence into adulthood, researchers can determine if smartphone addiction tends to persist or fluctuate over time. This information would be invaluable in identifying critical intervention periods to prevent or mitigate long-term adverse effects. Longitudinal studies can shed light on the impact of smartphone addiction on cognitive development. Through repeated assessments over several years, researchers can measure changes in cognitive functions such as attention span, memory, and decision-making skills. Longitudinal studies can also evaluate if these cognitive impairments are reversible or become permanent with prolonged smartphone addiction. This knowledge would aid in the development of effective interventions to improve these cognitive deficits and potentially prevent irreversible damage. Another crucial area that longitudinal studies can explore is the relationship between smartphone addiction and mental health outcomes. By repeatedly measuring mental health indicators such as depression, anxiety, and self-esteem, researchers can determine if smartphone addiction contributes to the development or worsening of these conditions over time. Understanding the long-term mental health consequences of smartphone addiction would enable clinicians to implement appropriate screening and treatment strategies, ultimately improving the overall well-being of individuals affected by excessive smartphone use. Longitudinal studies can also provide insight into the social implications of smartphone addiction. By following a cohort of individuals throughout their development, researchers can observe how smartphone addiction affects social interactions, relationships, and interpersonal skills over time. This information would be instrumental in devising strategies to prevent social isolation and cultivate healthy social habits in individuals at risk of smartphone addiction.

Another advantage of longitudinal studies is their ability to capture health-related outcomes associated with smartphone addiction. By continuously monitoring physical health parameters such as sleep quality, physical activity levels, and sedentary behaviors, researchers can determine if smartphone addiction contributes to the development of chronic health conditions, including obesity, cardiovascular diseases, and musculoskeletal disorders. This knowledge would support the implementation of preventive measures, such as educating individuals about the potential health risks and promoting a balanced lifestyle.

Longitudinal studies can offer insights into the economic

consequences of smartphone addiction. By assessing the academic and occupational outcomes of individuals with a history of smartphone addiction, researchers can determine if it leads to underachievement, decreased productivity, or limited career opportunities in the long run. Understanding the economic costs associated with smartphone addiction would allow policymakers to allocate resources effectively towards prevention and intervention programs. Longitudinal studies play a crucial role in assessing the long-term effects of smartphone addiction. By following individuals over an extended period, researchers can gather comprehensive data on the progression and stability of addiction, cognitive development, mental health outcomes, social implications, physical health consequences, and economic impacts. This knowledge is vital for developing effective strategies to combat smartphone abuse in children and adolescents, facilitating early intervention, and promoting healthier behaviors in the long term.

INVESTIGATING THE EFFICACY OF DIFFERENT INTERVENTION APPROACHES

In order to effectively combat smartphone addiction in children and adolescents, it is crucial to investigate the efficacy of various intervention approaches. One such approach is cognitive-behavioral therapy (CBT), which focuses on identifying and modifying maladaptive thoughts and behaviors. Research has shown that CBT can be effective in treating addictive behaviors, including internet and smartphone addiction. This therapeutic approach aims to enhance self-control, coping skills, and motivation to change through individual or group therapy sessions. A study conducted by Zhang et al. examined the effectiveness of CBT in reducing smartphone addiction among adolescents. The results indicated that participants who received CBT exhibited a significant decrease in smartphone addiction scores compared to those in the control group. This suggests that CBT may be a promising intervention approach for addressing smartphone addiction in this population. Another intervention approach that has shown promise in addressing smartphone addiction is mindfulness-based interventions (MBIs). MBIs, such as mindfulness-based cognitive therapy (MBCT) and mindfulness-based stress reduction (MBSR), aim to cultivate present-moment awareness and non-judgmental acceptance of thoughts and emotions. These interventions have been found to be effective in treating various mental health conditions, including addiction. A study conducted by Van Gordon et al. investigated the effects of a mindfulness-based intervention on smartphone addiction in young adults. The participants who received the intervention reported significant reductions in their smartphone addiction symptoms compared to the control group. These findings suggest that MBIs may be a valuable tool in addressing smartphone addiction in children and adolescents.

In addition to therapeutic interventions, educational programs targeting parents and schools can play a pivotal role in preventing and addressing smartphone addiction. Parental education programs can provide parents with valuable information about the risks and consequences of excessive smartphone use in children and strategies to set healthy boundaries. A study conducted by Lee et al. explored the effects of a parental education program on smartphone addiction in Korean adolescents. The results revealed that participants whose parents received the education program exhibited significant reductions in smartphone addiction scores compared to those in the control group. This highlights the importance of involving parents in intervention efforts to combat smartphone addiction. Similarly, school-based prevention programs can provide students with the knowledge and skills necessary to effectively manage their smartphone use. These programs often include psychoeducational workshops and interactive activities focused on fostering healthy digital habits. A study conducted by Conceição et al. examined the impact of a school-based prevention program on smartphone addiction in Portuguese adolescents. The findings showed that participants who participated in the program reported significant decreases in their smartphone addiction symptoms compared to those in the control group. These results indicate that school-based prevention programs may be an effective approach for addressing smartphone addiction in children and adolescents.

While these intervention approaches have shown promise in combating smartphone addiction, it is important to consider the limitations of the existing literature. Most studies have focused on short-term outcomes, and long-term efficacy remains uncertain. The majority of research has been conducted in Western countries, limiting the generalizability of the findings to other cultural contexts. The lack of standardized measures for assessing smartphone addiction makes it difficult to compare results across studies. Future research should aim to address these limitations by employing rigorous methodologies and exploring the effectiveness of intervention approaches in diverse populations.

Investigating the efficacy of different intervention approaches is crucial for effectively combatting smartphone addiction in children and adolescents. Cognitive-behavioral therapy and mindfulness-based interventions have shown promise in reducing smartphone addiction symptoms. Educational programs targeting parents and schools can also play a significant role in prevention and intervention efforts. Further research is needed to establish the long-term efficacy of these interventions and to explore their effectiveness in diverse populations. By adopting a comprehensive approach that combines therapeutic interventions, education, and prevention efforts, we can strive to mitigate the detrimental effects of smartphone addiction and promote healthy digital habits among children and adolescents.

EXAMINING THE INFLUENCE OF CULTURAL AND SOCIETAL FACTORS ON SMARTPHONE ABUSE

Cultural and societal factors play a significant role in shaping individuals' behaviors and attitudes towards smartphones, ultimately contributing to the problem of smartphone abuse among children and adolescents. One cultural factor that influences smartphone abuse is the prevailing belief in multitasking and constant connectivity. In today's fast-paced society, multitasking is often seen as a desirable skill, and smartphones enable individuals to juggle multiple tasks simultaneously. As a result, children and adolescents may feel pressure to constantly engage with their smartphones, checking notifications, responding to messages, and browsing social media feeds, even during activities that require their full attention. This cultural expectation fosters a mindset of constant connectivity, fueling smartphone abuse as individuals feel the need to be always available and connected digitally. Societal factors such as peer influence and social norms contribute to the problem of smartphone abuse. Adolescents are particularly vulnerable to peer pressure and the desire to fit in, and smartphones have become a prominent tool for social interaction and validation among this age group. The pressure to constantly check social media updates and respond to messages can be overwhelming, leading to excessive smartphone use and neglect of real-life relationships. The fear of missing out (FOMO) is another societal factor that influences smartphone abuse among children and adolescents. Social media platforms showcase curated and idealized versions of people's lives, creating a constant stream of envy-inducing posts. As a result, individuals may develop a fear of missing out on exciting events or experiences, leading them to spend excessive amounts of time on their smartphones, seeking validation and reassurance. Family dynamics and parenting styles also play a crucial role in smartphone abuse among children and adolescents. In some cultures, parents may use smartphones as a tool to keep their children occupied and entertained, inadvertently encouraging excessive screen time and dependence on smartphones. Parents' own smartphone use patterns can influence their children's behaviors. If parents are constantly engrossed in their devices, prioritizing virtual interactions over real-life interactions, children may internalize these behaviors and develop similar patterns of smartphone abuse. Inconsistent or lax parenting practices regarding smartphone use can contribute to excessive and unchecked smartphone usage among children and adolescents. The influence of cultural and societal factors extends beyond personal habits and behaviors to academic achievement. Today's education systems increasingly incorporate technology into classrooms, with students being encouraged to use smartphones and tablets for learning purposes. While technology can enhance the learning experience, the line between educational and recreational smartphone use can sometimes blur. As a result, children and adolescents may find themselves easily distracted by non-academic content, leading to decreased attention span, reduced productivity, and poorer academic performance. Cultural expectations regarding success and achievement can also contribute to smartphone abuse. In some societies, the pressure to perform well academically and excel in various extracurricular activities is immense. Students, especially adolescents, may believe that constant smartphone use is necessary to stay on top of their academic workload and maintain high grades. This desire to optimize productivity can often lead to a vicious cycle of smartphone dependency and reduced focus, thereby hindering academic success rather than enhancing it.

The influence of cultural and societal factors on smartphone abuse among children and adolescents is profound. The prevalent belief in multitasking and constant connectivity, peer pressure, social norms, family dynamics, and parenting styles, as well as academic and achievement expectations, all contribute to the problem. To combat smartphone abuse effectively, it is essential to understand and address these cultural and societal influences. Educating children, adolescents, and their families about healthy smartphone use, promoting balanced digital lifestyles, and creating supportive social and familial environments are crucial steps towards mitigating the negative impacts of smartphone abuse. Policymakers, educators, and parents must work together to establish guidelines and frameworks that foster responsible smartphone use among children and adolescents, ensuring that smartphones remain a beneficial tool rather than a detrimental addiction.

IDENTIFYING INDIVIDUAL DIFFERENCES THAT MAY CONTRIBUTE TO VULNERABILITY OR RESILIENCE

Identifying the individual differences that contribute to vulnerability or resilience to smartphone addiction is crucial in order to develop effective strategies to combat this pervasive issue. Firstly, it is important to acknowledge that certain personality traits or characteristics may render individuals more susceptible to developing smartphone addiction. Extroverted individuals, for example, may have a greater need for stimulation and may be more likely to engage in excessive smartphone use to satisfy this need. Individuals with low self-esteem may utilize smartphones as a means of escape or self-validation, leading to a heightened vulnerability to addiction. Individuals with underlying mental health disorders such as anxiety or depression may be more prone to seeking solace in their smartphones, thereby increasing their susceptibility to addiction. On the other hand, certain individual differences may contribute to resilience against smartphone addiction. For instance, individuals with high levels of self-control may be better equipped to resist the temptations of excessive smartphone use. They are more likely to set and adhere to boundaries regarding their phone usage, thus reducing their vulnerability to addiction. Individuals with strong support systems, whether it be from family, friends, or mentors, may have a greater sense of belonging and fulfillment in their offline interactions, reducing the need to rely solely on their smartphones for social validation or entertainment. Individuals with a high degree of self-awareness may be more cognizant of their smartphone use patterns and potential detrimental effects, consequently making conscious efforts to moderate their usage.

In addition to personality traits, demographic factors must also be considered in identifying individual differences that contribute to vulnerability or resilience to smartphone addiction. For instance, age plays a significant role in determining an individual's susceptibility to addiction. Research suggests that adolescents may be more vulnerable to smartphone addiction due to their developmental stage characterized by increased impulsivity and susceptibility to peer influences. Individuals from lower socioeconomic backgrounds may be at higher risk for addiction due to limited access to alternative recreational activities or lack of parental supervision. Conversely, individuals from higher socioeconomic backgrounds may possess greater resources to combat addiction, such as access to therapy or extracurricular activities that promote healthy habits and social interactions.

Cultural factors also play a key role in shaping individual differences in vulnerability to smartphone addiction. For instance, in collectivist cultures where group conformity and social harmony are highly valued, individuals may be more susceptible to peer pressure and may feel compelled to engage in excessive smartphone use to fit in or stay connected. On the other hand, individualistic cultures that prioritize independence and personal autonomy may foster a greater sense of self-control and resilience against smartphone addiction.

It is worth noting that while certain individual differences may predispose individuals to vulnerability or resilience to smartphone addiction, they should not be viewed as fixed traits. Rather, they exist on a continuum and can be molded and influenced by various external factors. For instance, individuals who are initially vulnerable to addiction due to low self-esteem may develop resilience through therapy or self-help strategies that enhance their self-esteem and self-worth. Similarly, individuals who possess high levels of self-control but lack awareness of the potential risks of smartphone addiction may benefit from targeted education or interventions that enhance their knowledge and understanding of this issue. Identifying individual differences that contribute to vulnerability or resilience to smartphone addiction is vital in order to develop targeted strategies to combat this growing problem. Personality traits, such as extroversion or self-control, as well as demographic factors, such as age and socioeconomic status, all play a role in shaping an individual's susceptibility to addiction. Cultural factors can further influence an individual's vulnerability or resilience to smartphone addiction. It is essential to recognize that these individual differences are not static and can be influenced by external factors, allowing for the possibility of intervention and prevention. By understanding and addressing these individual differences, we can work towards creating a healthier digital environment for children and adolescents. Screen addiction is a growing phenomenon among children and adolescents, posing significant challenges for parents, educators, and mental health professionals. With the widespread availability and constant accessibility of smartphones, this addiction has become increasingly prevalent, affecting individuals' daily lives and overall well-being. A multitude of strategies can be employed to combat smartphone abuse in this vulnerable population, considering both prevention and treatment avenues. Firstly, promoting awareness and education about the risks and consequences associated with excessive smartphone use is crucial. Parents and educators should actively engage in discussions with children and adolescents, emphasizing the importance of balance and healthy technology habits. By fostering open dialogues, young individuals can gain a better understanding of the negative impact of extensive smartphone use on their cognitive, social, and emotional development. Setting clear boundaries and establishing consistent rules regarding smartphone usage is essential. Parents need to enforce such guidelines, ensuring that screen time remains limited and specific to designated periods. Parental control applications, which restrict access to certain applications or content, can also be utilized as a way to uphold these boundaries. Equally important is providing alternative activities and opportunities for children and adolescents to engage in. Encouraging physical exercise, outdoor adventures, and hobbies that do not involve screens can help shift their focus away from smartphone dependency. Fostering interpersonal connections through family time, social activities, and face-to-face conversations can encourage meaningful relationships and diminish the need for excessive virtual interactions. Another effective strategy to combat smartphone abuse is emphasizing the importance of quality sleep. Research has consistently demonstrated that excessive smartphone use, particularly prior to bedtime, can disrupt the sleep-wake cycle, leading to sleep deprivation and other related health issues. Parents and educators should educate and emphasize the significance of establishing consistent sleep routines and implementing technology-free bedrooms to create optimal sleep environments. Alongside prevention strategies, various treatment approaches can be employed to address smartphone addiction in children and adolescents. Cognitive-behavioral therapy (CBT) can be an effective tool in helping individuals modify their maladaptive thoughts, behaviors, and beliefs associated with smartphone abuse. This therapeutic intervention aims to challenge cognitive distortions, develop coping mechanisms, and promote healthier technology use habits. In addition to CBT, mindfulness-based techniques, such as meditation and relaxation exercises, can aid in fostering self-awareness and impulse control. By practicing mindfulness, individuals can learn to observe their thoughts and urges without judgment, allowing them to break free from their smartphone addiction. Family therapy can also play a pivotal role in the treatment of smartphone abuse. By involving family members in therapy sessions, parents and siblings can gain a better understanding of the addiction and its impact. This collaborative approach enables family members to provide support and learn effective ways to manage and balance smartphone usage within the household. Psychological interventions can be complemented with the use of digital detox programs and support groups specifically tailored to address smartphone addiction. These programs often include a combination of educational sessions, counseling, and peer support, creating a supportive environment for individuals to share their experiences and strategies for recovery. Combatting smartphone abuse in children and adolescents requires a comprehensive approach that encompasses prevention and treatment strategies. By promoting awareness, establishing clear boundaries, encouraging alternative activities, and emphasizing the importance of quality sleep, parents, educators, and mental health professionals can mitigate the detrimental effects of excessive smartphone use. Implementing evidence-based treatment approaches, such as cognitive-behavioral therapy, mindfulness techniques, and family therapy, can further support individuals in overcoming their addiction and developing healthier technology habits. It is imperative that we address screen addiction promptly and effectively, considering the profound impact it can have on the well-being and development of our younger generation.

IX. CONCLUSION

It is evident that smartphone abuse among children and adolescents is a growing concern that requires immediate attention. As technology continues to advance, it becomes essential for parents, educators, and policymakers to implement strategies to combat this issue effectively. While smartphones offer numerous benefits and opportunities for learning and communication, they can also have detrimental effects on the mental, physical, and social well-being of young individuals. It is crucial to establish a balance between the usage of smartphones and engaging in other activities that promote face-to-face interactions, physical exercise, and a healthy lifestyle. To address smartphone addiction, both parents and schools can play a significant role by promoting awareness and education regarding this issue. Parents should be encouraged to limit their child's screen time and set clear rules and boundaries regarding smartphone usage. By modeling healthy phone habits, parents can teach their children the importance of moderation and self-control. Parents should be involved in their child's digital life, monitoring the content they consume, and discussing the potential risks of excessive smartphone use. Schools, on the other hand, can incorporate digital literacy programs in their curriculum, teaching students about the impact of excessive smartphone use and providing them with strategies to manage their screen time effectively. By integrating technology responsibly into the curriculum, educators can help students develop a healthy relationship with their smartphones and encourage them to use digital devices as tools for learning rather than sources of distraction. Schools can promote outdoor activities and extracurricular programs that encourage physical exercise, creativity, and interpersonal connections. By creating a balanced environment that offers alternative activities, schools can help diminish the appeal of excessive smartphone usage. Policymakers have a crucial role in implementing regulations and guidelines to protect children and adolescents from smartphone addiction. Governments can work closely with technology companies to develop software features that limit screen time and promote healthy smartphone usage. By mandating the inclusion of such features in smartphones, policymakers can help mitigate the negative consequences of excessive smartphone use. Policymakers should focus on enacting policies that restrict the advertisement and marketing of smartphones towards children and adolescents. By reducing the exposure to targeted advertisements, policymakers can reduce the influence of marketing tactics that contribute to smartphone addiction. Combating smartphone abuse among children and adolescents requires a collaborative effort from parents, educators, and policymakers. By establishing clear boundaries, promoting awareness, and integrating alternative activities, parents can provide their children with a balanced lifestyle that goes beyond smartphone dependence. Schools, in turn, should incorporate digital literacy programs and create an environment that encourages face-to-face interactions and physical exercise. Policymakers must regulate smartphone usage and ensure that technology companies prioritize the well-being of children and adolescents over profit. By working together, we can combat smartphone addiction and create a healthier, more balanced future for our youth.

RECAP OF THE IMPORTANCE OF SMARTPHONE ABUSE IN CHILDREN AND ADOLESCENTS

Addressing smartphone abuse in children and adolescents is of paramount importance. As technology continues to advance and smartphones become an integral part of our daily lives, the negative consequences of excessive smartphone use cannot be ignored. The detrimental effects on physical health, mental well-being, and academic performance highlight the urgent need for intervention strategies. From a physical perspective, prolonged smartphone use can contribute to obesity, musculoskeletal problems, and sleep disturbances. This is further compounded by the negative impact on mental health, including increased rates of anxiety, depression, and loneliness. Excessive smartphone use has been linked to poor academic performance, with students experiencing decreased attention span, reduced cognitive abilities, and limited ability to retain information.

Although some might argue that banning smartphones altogether is the solution, this approach fails to recognize the importance of technology in the modern era. Smartphones can provide valuable educational resources and enhance communication. Instead, it is crucial to promote healthy smartphone habits and develop effective strategies to combat abuse.

One approach is to increase awareness and education around the risks associated with smartphone abuse. Parents, educators, and healthcare professionals should be equipped with the knowledge to identify and address problematic smartphone use in children and adolescents. This could involve educational programs in schools, workshops for parents, and training for healthcare providers. By educating individuals about the potential consequences, they can make informed decisions and support young people in establishing healthy smartphone habits.

Another important strategy is to establish clear boundaries and guidelines surrounding smartphone use. Setting limits on screen time, such as a maximum number of hours per day, can help prevent excessive usage. Implementing technology-free zones or designated times when smartphones are not allowed can promote healthier habits and encourage individuals to engage in other activities. It is also important for parents and caregivers to lead by example and demonstrate responsible smartphone use themselves. By creating a culture where technology is used mindfully and in moderation, children and adolescents are more likely to adopt healthy habits. It is essential to cultivate alternative activities and hobbies that can replace excessive smartphone use. Encouraging physical activity, social interaction, and creative endeavors can help divert attention away from screens. Schools can play a critical role in providing extracurricular activities that foster personal growth and development beyond the digital realm. This could include sports teams, art clubs, music programs, and community service opportunities. By creating a supportive environment that promotes diverse interests and passions, young people are less likely to rely solely on smartphones for entertainment and engagement. In addition to these strategies, incorporating technology management apps and features can assist in regulating smartphone usage. There are numerous applications and settings available that enable parents to monitor and control their children's smartphone use. These tools can help enforce screen time limits, block certain apps or websites, and track overall usage. By utilizing these resources, parents can regain control and promote responsible smartphone habits.

Fostering open communication and dialogue is crucial in addressing smartphone abuse. Parents, educators, and healthcare professionals should create safe spaces where children and adolescents can openly discuss their smartphone use and any challenges they may be facing. By listening non-judgmentally and offering guidance and support, young people will feel comfortable seeking help when needed. This can facilitate early intervention and prevent the escalation of problematic smartphone use.

The importance of addressing smartphone abuse in children and adolescents cannot be overstated. The negative impact on physical health, mental well-being, and academic performance necessitates the implementation of effective strategies. By increasing awareness, setting clear boundaries, promoting alternative activities, utilizing technology management tools, and fostering open communication, we can combat smartphone abuse and help young people develop healthy relationships with technology. It is our collective responsibility to guide and support the next generation in navigating the digital world.

EMPHASIZING OF STRATEGIES TO COMBAT SMARTPHONE ADDICTION

The issue of smartphone addiction among children and adolescents is complex and requires a multi-faceted approach to address effectively. One strategy that should be emphasized is raising awareness about the potential harms of excessive smartphone use. Educating parents, teachers, and youth about the detrimental effects of smartphone addiction can help prevent its onset and prompt early intervention.

This can be done through various means, such as workshops, seminars, and public health campaigns. By highlighting the negative consequences, such as impaired mental health, poor academic performance, and weakened social relationships, individuals can become more wary of their smartphone use and take steps to curb their addiction. Emphasizing the importance of parental involvement is crucial in combating smartphone addiction. Parents play a vital role in shaping their child's behavior and should be actively involved in monitoring their smartphone usage. Creating open lines of communication within the family can contribute to a healthier relationship with smartphones. Establishing rules and boundaries, such as screen-free zones and scheduled screen time, can help regulate smartphone use and prevent excessive reliance. Parents should also model healthy smartphone habits themselves, as children often emulate their parents' behavior. By demonstrating responsible smartphone use, parents can set a positive example for their children to follow. Incorporating technology breaks into daily routines can help break the cycle of smartphone addiction. Encouraging children and adolescents to engage in alternative activities, such as outdoor play, sports, arts, and hobbies, can redirect their attention away from smartphones. Providing opportunities for socialization and face-to-face interactions is essential in developing healthy interpersonal skills and decreasing reliance on virtual connections. Schools can also play a role in promoting technology breaks by implementing policies that limit smartphone use during class hours and encouraging extracurricular activities that foster offline engagement. In addition to these preventative measures, incorporating psychological interventions can be beneficial in combating smartphone addiction. Cognitive-behavioral therapy (CBT) has shown promise in addressing addictive behaviors. CBT can help individuals identify negative thought patterns and develop healthier coping mechanisms to regulate their smartphone use. Group therapy sessions, where individuals can share experiences and provide support for one another, can be particularly effective in fostering behavior change. Mindfulness-based interventions have been found to reduce smartphone addiction by promoting present-moment awareness and reducing cravings for constant connectivity. These therapeutic approaches can contribute to long-term behavior change and provide individuals with the tools to manage their smartphone use.

Addressing the systemic factors contributing to smartphone addiction is crucial to combat this issue effectively. Technology companies should be held accountable for designing products that encourage addictive behaviors. Implementing regulations that promote ethical design principles, such as limiting notifications and creating user-friendly interfaces, can contribute to reducing smartphone addiction. Social media platforms should take responsibility for fostering a healthy online environment by introducing features that promote meaningful interactions and discourage comparison and self-esteem issues. By recognizing the role of the industry in perpetuating smartphone addiction, society can work towards creating a healthier digital landscape. Combating smartphone addiction requires a collaborative effort from various stakeholders, including educators, healthcare professionals, policymakers, and parents. Establishing interdisciplinary partnerships is essential in developing comprehensive strategies that address the multifaceted nature of smartphone addiction. Research initiatives and funding should be directed towards understanding the underlying mechanisms of smartphone addiction and identifying effective interventions. Policymakers should work towards creating policies that promote digital literacy and regulate marketing practices targeting children and adolescents. By working together, these stakeholders can contribute to a society that fosters healthy smartphone usage habits and mitigates the negative impacts of smartphone addiction.

Combatting smartphone addiction in children and adolescents necessitates a multi-faceted approach that addresses various aspects of this complex issue. Raising awareness, involving parents, incorporating technology breaks, providing psychological interventions, addressing systemic factors, and fostering interdisciplinary collaborations are all vital strategies in mitigating smartphone addiction. By employing these strategies, society can promote a healthier relationship with smartphones and empower the younger generation to navigate the digital world responsibly.

COLLABORATION BETWEEN PARENTS, SCHOOLS, COMMUNITIES, AND HEALTHCARE PROFESSIONALS TO TACKLE THIS ISSUE

In order to effectively combat smartphone abuse in children and adolescents, it is imperative that a call for collaboration is made between parents, schools, communities, and healthcare professionals. The complexity of this issue requires a multifaceted approach that combines the efforts and expertise of these key stakeholders. First and foremost, parents play a critical role in addressing smartphone addiction in their children. They must be actively engaged in their child's life and monitor their smartphone usage. By setting clear boundaries and establishing tech-free zones at home, parents can help create a healthy balance between technology and other activities. Parents should educate themselves about the potential dangers of smartphone addiction, such as cyberbullying and online predators, and teach their children about responsible smartphone usage.

Schools also have a vital role in addressing smartphone abuse among students. They can incorporate digital literacy programs into the curriculum, teaching students about the potential risks of excessive smartphone use and ways to develop healthy screen-time habits. Schools should also collaborate with parents to develop policies and guidelines for smartphone use during school hours, ensuring that educational time is not compromised by excessive screen time. Communities, including neighborhood associations, community centers, and local organizations, can contribute to combating smartphone addiction by organizing and hosting educational workshops and awareness campaigns. These initiatives can raise awareness about the consequences of excessive smartphone use and provide parents and children with practical tools and strategies to manage screen time effectively. By fostering a sense of community, individuals can support each other in addressing smartphone addiction, sharing experiences, and seeking guidance. Healthcare professionals have a crucial role in identifying and treating smartphone addiction. Mental health professionals should be trained to recognize the signs and symptoms of smartphone addiction and provide appropriate interventions. This includes individual counseling, family therapy, and support groups tailored to address the specific challenges associated with excessive smartphone use.

Healthcare professionals should collaborate with schools and parents to develop screening tools to identify individuals at risk of smartphone addiction, enabling early intervention and prevention. Collaboration among parents, schools, communities, and healthcare professionals can provide a comprehensive approach to tackling smartphone addiction in children and adolescents. By combining their efforts, these stakeholders can pool resources, knowledge, and experiences to develop effective strategies and interventions. This collaboration can help overcome the challenges that may arise when addressing this issue. Each stakeholder brings a unique perspective and expertise that can contribute to a holistic understanding of smartphone addiction and its impact on children and adolescents. By working together, these stakeholders can develop evidence-based interventions that consider the individual needs of children and adolescents, as well as the broader social and cultural contexts in which they operate. For instance, parents can share their experiences and observations with schools, providing valuable insights that can inform educational initiatives and policies. Similarly, communities can serve as a support network for parents, facilitating dialogue and the exchange of best practices. Healthcare professionals, on the other hand, can contribute their expertise in understanding addiction and mental health, ensuring that interventions are evidence-based and effective.

Addressing smartphone addiction in children and adolescents requires a collaborative effort between parents, schools, communities, and healthcare professionals. By working together, these stakeholders can develop comprehensive strategies to prevent, identify, and treat smartphone addiction. Through educational initiatives, policy development, and the provision of mental health support, this collaborative approach can empower children and adolescents to develop healthy screen-time habits and navigate the digital world responsibly. Collaboration is key to effectively combating smartphone abuse and promoting the well-being of our youth.

BIBLIOGRAPHY

Aukasz Wojtasik. 'Protecting Children Against Corporal Punishment.' Awareness-raising Campaigns, Monika Sajkowska, Council of Europe, 1/1/2004

Vladan Starcevic. 'Mental Health in the Digital Age.' Grave Dangers, Great Promise, Elias Aboujaoude, Oxford University Press, 1/1/2015